INTERNATIONAL JOURNAL OF PSYCHOLOGY, 2006, 41 (4), 241–242

Preface

T0349526

Special issue on the indigenous psychologies

Carl Martin Allwood

Lund University, Sweden

John W. Berry

Queen's University, Kingston, Canada

The indigenous psychologies are an interesting new phenomenon in psychology. They illustrate a questioning and decentring of Western-dominated psychological research. How these new psychologies should be characterized is very much an open question. However, indigenous psychologies may be described as a set of approaches to understanding human behaviour within the cultural contexts in which they have developed and are currently displayed. They can also be seen as attempts to root psychological research in the conceptual systems that are indigenous to a culture, including the philosophical, theological, and scientific ideas that are part of the historical and contemporary lives of people and their institutions.

The recent development of indigenous psychologies in their many forms presents both a challenge to, and the possibility for renewal of, mainstream psychology. For example, indigenous psychologies promise to provide information and insights into new phenomena that might have been difficult to identify without them. Thus, indigenous psychologies are likely to lead to discovery of new aspects of reality. Furthermore, indigenous psychologies are of interest not only for psychology, but also, for example, for anthropology and philosophy, since at least some versions of indigenous psychologies involve attempts to question descriptive categories for phenomena as well as methodologies, forms, and values of science that are usually taken for granted.

Another feature of indigenous psychologies is their wide variety. They now differ among themselves and it is possible that they will differ even more in the future. It is not clear whether common denominators will eventually be established for all or most forms of indigenous psychologies.

This special issue aims to present a sample of thinking about, and current research on, indigenous psychologies. It includes a core article by Allwood and Berry (with contributions by other authors). This article provides a picture of the current conceptions of 15 leading researchers in the indigenous psychologies field. They were asked to give their views on how the indigenous psychologies originated globally and in their own country. We also asked them to give their views on what the important characteristics of indigenized psychologies are on the global, world level, and in their own country today. The editors then discuss these contributions in terms of 8 important themes that we discerned in the 15 contributions. Among the many conclusions were that the indigenous psychologies show both homogeneity (for example with respect to their critique of Western-dominated mainstream psychology) and heterogeneity (for example with respect to the research methodology used). There is also an important tension within indigenous psychologies with respect to the degree to which they identify themselves with what is commonly called "cultural psychology."

The distinguished historian of psychology, Kurt Danziger, then provides an article that comments on the main paper. He discusses the indigenous psychologies with respect to science, discipline, and voice, thus putting them into a broader context.

http://www.psypress.com/ijp

DOI: 10.1080/00207590544000022

The last set of contributions to this special issue provide examples of ongoing research programmes into indigenous psychologies in various parts of the world. Although most contributions come from East Asia, this reflects the current active research work going on in this region. There is also much important work on indigenous psychologies taking place in other cultures. Despite our attempts to involve scholars from other regions, we were not able to sample their activities adequately. We hope that this special issue will spur further research and debate on indigenous psychologies in all parts of the world.

This special issue on Indigenous Psychologies is dedicated to the memory of Professor Rogelio Diaz Guerrero, whose life work contributed so much to the understanding of indigenous approaches to human behaviour.

INTERNATIONAL JOURNAL OF PSYCHOLOGY, 2006, 41 (4), 243–268

Origins and development of indigenous psychologies: An international analysis

Carl Martin Allwood

Lund University, Sweden

John W. Berry

Queen's University, Kingston, Canada

With contributions by: Carl Martin Allwood; John Berry; Pawel Boski; Fanny M. Cheung; Kwang-Kuo Hwang; Henry Kao; Uichol Kim & Young-Shin Park; Leo Marai; Fathali M. Moghaddam; Linda Waimarie Nikora, Michelle Levy, Bridgette Masters, & Moana Waitoki; A. Bame Nsamenang; Elizabeth Protacio-De Castro (formerly Marcelino), Melecio C. Fabros, & Reginald Kapunan; T. S. Saraswathi; Jai B. P. Sinha; Kuo-Shu Yang

*T*his article examines the origin, development, and characteristics of the indigenous psychologies (IPs) initiated in various regions of the world. These IPs arose as a reaction to the mainstream version of psychology and seek to reflect the social, political, and cultural character of peoples around the world. Fifteen contributions from researchers from different parts of the world are presented, replying to four questions that were posed to them. A number of common themes were identified in the contributions. Post-colonial reactions to mainstream psychology, and the belief that it was not an efficient aid to solving local social problems, were seen as important reasons for developing IPs. IPs were generally seen as attempts to produce a local psychology within a specific cultural context. Different views about what methods are legitimate in IPs were present (from experiments to various more "humanistic" methods). IPs were commonly seen as being able to open up, invigorate, and improve mainstream psychology. The style of theorizing in the IPs was felt by many to be to build theories from the "bottom up" on the basis of local phenomena, findings, and experiences. Some contributors saw the IP as a kind of cultural psychology, and a few noted that IP and cross-cultural psychology have an interactive mutually enriching relationship. Nearly half of the contributors emphasized the critical reaction to their work on IP by colleagues working more in the line of mainstream psychology. Many contributors felt that IP could contribute to the development of a more general universal psychology. Different indications of heterogeneity in the IPs were found among the contributors, for example, with respect to the role given to religion in the local IP. Sometimes the presence of different IPs within the same country was reported. This also indicates heterogeneity in the IPs.

*C*et article examine l'origine, le développement et les caractéristiques des psychologies indigènes (PIs) initiées dans plusieurs régions du monde. Ces PIs ont émergé en réaction à la version dominante de la psychologie et cherchaient à refléter le caractère social, politique et culturel des individus autour du monde. Quinze contributions de chercheurs de différentes parties du monde sont présentées. Ces chercheurs répondent à quatre questions qui leur ont été posées. Un certain nombre de thèmes communs furent identifiés dans les contributions. Les réactions post-coloniales vis-à-vis la psychologie dominante et la croyance qu'il ne s'agissait pas d'une aide efficace pour résoudre des problèmes sociaux locaux furent soulevées comme étant des raisons importantes pour développer les PIs. Les PIs étaient généralement perçues comme des tentatives de produire une psychologie locale dans un contexte culturel spécifique. Des points de vue différents sur les méthodes considérées comme légitimes dans les PIs étaient présentées (des expérimentations à une variété de méthodes plus «humanistes»). Les PIs étaient communément perçues comme étant capables d'ouvrir, de revigorer et d'améliorer la psychologie dominante. Plusieurs ont exprimé que la façon de faire des théories dans les PIs consiste à construire des théories à partir de la base en fonction de phénomènes, d'expériences et de résultats locaux. Certains collaborateurs voyaient les PIs comme une sorte de psychologie culturelle et quelques-uns ont noté que la PI et la psychologie trans-culturelle ont une relation interactive mutuellement enrichissante. Près de la moitié des collaborateurs ont mis l'emphase sur la réaction critique de leurs travaux sur la PI de la part de collègues travaillant davantage en fonction de la psychologie dominante. Plusieurs collaborateurs croyaient que la PI peut contribuer au développement d'une psychologie générale davantage universelle. Différentes indications de l'hétérogénéité dans

Correspondence should be addressed to Carl Martin Allwood, Dept of Psychology, Lund University, Box 213, SE-221 00 Lund, Sweden (e-mail: cma@psychology.lu.se) or to John Berry (e-mail: berryj@king.igs.net).

DOI: 10.1080/00207590544000013

les PIs ont été trouvées dans les contributions, par exemple, en regard du rôle donné à la religion dans la PI locale. Quelques fois, la présence de différentes PIs dans un même pays était rapportée. Ceci illustre aussi l'hétérogénéité dans les PIs.

*E*ste artículo analiza el origen, el desarrollo y las características de las psicologías tradicionales (PT) iniciadas en zonas diversas del mundo. Estas PT surgieron en respuesta a la versión dominante de la psicología e intentan reflejar el carácter social, político y cultural de los pueblos de todo el mundo. Aquí se presentan quince artículos de investigadores de diferentes partes del mundo que responden a cuatro preguntas que se les plantearon. Los artículos incluyeron varios temas comunes. Las reacciones post-coloniales ante la psicología dominante, y la creencia de que ésta no representaba una ayuda eficaz para resolver los problemas sociales locales, constituyeron buenas razones para que se desarrollaran las PT. En términos generales, las PT se consideraron intentos por producir una psicología local dentro de un contexto cultural específico. Hubo diferentes opiniones respecto a cuáles métodos eran legítimos dentro de las PT (desde experimentos hasta varios métodos más 'humanísticos'). En general se creía que las PT podían abrir, vigorizar y mejorar la psicología dominante. Para muchos, la manera de crear teorías en las PT consistía en construir teorías a partir de la base, en función de fenómenos, de experiencias y resultados locales. Algunos colaboradores vieron en las PT una especie de psicología cultural, y algunos notaron que las PT y la psicología transcultural guardan una relación interactiva mutuamente enriquecedora. Casi la mitad de los colaboradores subrayaron la reacción crítica que hacia sus trabajos sobre las PT mostraban colegas que trabajaban más dentro de los lineamientos de la psicología dominante. Varios de los colaboradores sentían que las PT podían contribuir al desarrollo de una psicología universal más general. Los colaboradores hallaron distintos indicios de heterogeneidad de las PT, por ejemplo en lo que respecta al papel que se le ha dado a la religión en las PT locales. En ocasiones se reportó la presencia de diferentes PT dentro de un mismo país. Esto es un indicio de heterogeneidad en las PT.

In this article we are concerned with the issue of the origin and development of indigenous psychologies[1] in various regions of the world. Specifically, we search for the conditions and processes that underlie the emergence of psychologies that seek to reflect the social, political, and cultural character of peoples around the world. We sought to accomplish this by asking colleagues to reflect on these questions, and then by presenting our analyses of their responses. Following a brief introduction to the field, we present 15 replies to our questions, and conclude with a discussion of the similarities and differences in views about IPs (indigenous psychologies).

It is generally agreed that human behaviour is shaped by the cultural context in which it developed. We can view the discipline of psychology as a complex set of behaviours (including concepts, methods, and interpretations) that emerged in one cultural region of the world (the European-American). These behaviours had their roots mainly in one religio-philosophical tradition (the Judeo-Christian), and had been passed on to the West mainly by one thought-tradition (the Greco-Roman). The outcome is the widespread presence of one indigenous psychology (that of Western societies), which has been exported to, and largely accepted by, other societies.

The IP approach to psychology has developed in many different countries and continents in the last 30 years or so and represents an important challenge to the mainstream[2], mainly Western, psychology (WP). The IP approach can be characterized as attempts by researchers in mostly non-Western societies and cultures to develop a psychological science that more closely reflects their own social and cultural premises. Thus, by their own self-understanding, these psychologies

---

[1]There are at least two possible terms with which to label the psychologies discussed in this article: "indigenous" psychologies and "indigenized" psychologies. Both terms have merit, but both can be criticized. For example, the label "indigenous psychology" risks creating confusion with older cultural traditions often stemming from religion and philosophy in a country, such as ideas put forth in Hindu philosophy or religion regarding human beings. Although the psychologies we focus on certainly draw on such traditions, they rarely or never identify themselves totally with these traditions. Moreover, these psychologies are at least to some extent a reaction to (and at the same time often also partly inspired by) mainstream Western psychology. The label "indigenized psychologies" has the drawback that it may be interpreted as implying that the process of indigenizing is completed. However, like all scientific traditions, they are continuously developing. Another drawback with using "indigenized psychology" is that it can be interpreted to overemphasize their dependency on Western psychology. Since the term "indigenous psychology" is the one commonly used in the literature we will keep that usage here. Henceforth, we use "IP" to refer to them.

[2]When we talk about mainstream psychology, we do not want to imply that this psychology has some higher or central status among the different approaches to psychology. What we mean by this label (and also by "Western psychology"), is that this is one specific tradition with its own characteristics, and which today is the largest psychological tradition. Henceforth, we use "WP" to refer to it.

reflect, just as WP (Western mainstream psychology) does, their own social and cultural contexts.

The IPs should be distinguished from other forms of culture-oriented psychologies such as cross-cultural psychology and cultural psychology (see, e.g., Hwang & Yang, 2000). Cross-cultural psychology typically has a comparative perspective (see, e.g., Berry, Poortinga, Segall, & Dasen, 2002) and cultural psychology a perspective inspired by the activity theory created by Soviet psychologists (Vygotsky, Leontiev, and others) and writings in social anthropology (see, e.g., Cole, 1996). The IPs are distinguished from these other approaches by their determination to use their own cultural resources in their development of the psychological discipline.

Such an approach to science constitutes a breach with a traditional view of science as neutral and objective. However, although many observers see merit in the 20th-century positivistic norm that science should be objective and independent of politics and religion, later developments in the study of science (for example in the area of science studies) have demonstrated the dependence between science as it is practised and the society in which it is produced (e.g., Giere, 1992; Mulkay, 1972; Shadish & Fuller, 1994; Ziman, 1995, 2000). The problems researched, the methods by which they are studied, and the type of arguments counted as relevant, valid, and legitimate to support the researchers' conclusions are all seen as dependent on culturally dependent pre-understanding.

Taking a general approach to this issue, even if we recognize the cultural dependency of research—and more specifically of psychology—this still does not solve the more normative issue concerning what types of cultural pre-understandings should be welcomed, or allowed to play a role in, research (see, e.g., Taylor, 1996). It can be seen in the great variety of answers to this issue given the different specific IPs that this is an unresolved issue in these psychologies. For example, the question concerning the role to be given to religious understanding in the IPs is not answered in a uniform way.

There are two questions concerning the IP approach: the extent to which the goal to intentionally create a psychology from one's own social conditions and cultural understandings is compatible with norms about the objectivity in science; and the extent to which it is desirable to achieve such objectivity in research. Both these questions have given impetus to the ongoing development of the IPs. Given our position that WP is also an indigenous one (because it is dependent on its own cultural background), such questions are of equal relevance for WP.

There are many reasons why the IPs are of interest. Each IP provides a new and different perspective from which to gain understanding of the human being. Thus, by intentionally using their cultural context as a starting point for their own development, the IPs have made possible a multiple expansion of the possibilities to improve our understanding of mankind. In addition, the premise subscribed to in the IPs that they, and all other approaches to psychology, are rooted in and relative to their cultural background, poses a significant challenge to WP's traditional self-image of being neutral and objective. By perceiving itself as a culturally dependent, locally-originated indigenous psychology, WP may achieve a more realistic self-image.

Furthermore, because the development of the IPs has incorporated the notion of their cultural contingency into their self-understanding, they provide an informative and provocative example of how such awareness is handled in a research tradition. An intriguing facet here is how the specific IPs relate to the notion of science. For example, to what extent will the IPs attempt to revise, or distance themselves from, traditional notions of science?

An improved understanding of the nature of IP as a constitutive phenomenon (i.e., as a process wherein understanding of the human being is generated) will provide a better understanding about the nature of human knowledge development, and more specifically about the conditions and possibilities for psychological understanding of the human being. In this context, the question of the *origin* of the psychologies in the IP approach is of great interest. Generally speaking, understanding the origins of a phenomenon provides insight into its background conditions and this, in turn, provides information about the type of phenomenon dealt with. Thus, a better understanding of the origins of the IPs may improve our understanding of the IP approach.

In addition, a better understanding of the origins of IPs provides insight into the processes of the social production of understanding, in this case of understanding generated in a scientific framework. For example, it is of relevance to analyse to what extent the different IPs originated independently in their own cultural contexts, and to what extent their creation was at least partly a consequence of a general *zeitgeist* and impulses from the international academic arena.

There are different ways to investigate the issues raised above. One way to learn more about what characterizes the IPs, and about their origins, is to ask researchers involved in this approach. Such an approach will provide the informed views of the relevant involved actors. Different researchers are likely to answer the questions in different ways; the degree of heterogeneity in the answers is informative with respect to the diversity among the IPs. Moreover, the answers given by different authors about the characteristics and origins of the IPs are also of interest, since they reflect how the different authors choose to strategically position themselves in the rhetorical arena with respect to the phenomena in question (e.g., Borofsky, 1987; Middleton & Edwards, 1990).

On a more practical level, we attempted to identify the most relevant actors in the field and to ask them to provide their answers to four questions (presented below). We used two criteria for the selection of contributing researchers: (1) to achieve global spread, and (2) to include important/interesting researchers in the field. Initially we sent out a letter of invitation to 20 prominent researchers in the IPs asking them to contribute their answers to our questions. These letters were sent to researchers in all regions of the world. Of those invited, three did not answer (despite reminders), three declined to participate (because they did not consider themselves appropriate respondents), and two agreed to participate, but despite reminders, did not. One further contribution was invited and accepted along the way. Many of the texts contributed were longer than the length stated in the invitation (800 words). We edited these texts and these are included in the present paper with the contributors' approval.

The four questions we asked the contributors to answer were the following:

1. Give a brief description of the history of the development of the indigenized psychologies globally (e.g., When did the indigenized psychologies start to develop globally? Where did the initiative come from? Name some significant event in the global development of the indigenized psychologies. Describe the approach taken and the important research questions formulated, as you see it, and name some of the important researchers.)
2. Give a brief description of the history of the development of the indigenized psychologies in your own country (e.g., When did the indigenized psychologies start to develop in your country and what relation did this development have to the global development of indigenized psychologies? Where did the initiative come from in your country? Name

some significant event in the development of the indigenized psychologies in your country. Describe the approach taken and the important research questions formulated, as you see it, and name some of the important researchers in your country. To what extent do you consider that an indigenized psychology approach [in contrast to US/Western mainstream psychological research] is dominating psychological research in your country?)
3. Describe briefly some important characteristics of the indigenized psychologies on the global world level, today.
4. Describe briefly some important characteristics of the indigenized psychologies in your own country today.

CONTRIBUTIONS

Fanny M. Cheung, Department of Psychology, Chinese University, Hong Kong, China

Global development and characteristics

Theories and constructs of psychology are developed in a cultural context; some are universally applicable, others may be more relevant to a particular cultural context. Psychology as an independent discipline began in Western cultures. With the dominance of Western psychology, there is an assumption that the existing theories are universal. Cross-cultural differences in research findings have identified "culture-bound" or indigenous phenomena, which were often viewed with curiosity but largely ignored in mainstream psychology. Early attempts to import and adapt Western theories and tools have given rise to concerns about their local relevance. Local psychologists have to choose between adapting to Western models or searching for their own theories and tools that provide more meaning. These indigenous approaches were mostly isolated from Western psychology.

With globalization as a social force in the 21st century, cross-cultural psychology is challenging these assumptions and practices, and raising the awareness that Western psychology may itself be an "indigenized" form of psychology. A more integrative approach is now combining the initial dichotomy of etic vs. emic approaches to consider how "universal" constructs may be manifested differently in different cultural contexts, and how "indigenous" constructs may be different ways of cutting the same psychological reality in different cultural contexts.

Country development and characteristics

The indigenization movement in Chinese psychology began in Taiwan in the 1970s. Kuo-Shu Yang pioneered the movement with a focus on important personality constructs in Chinese societies, including traditionalism-modernity and social orientation. He and his associates developed a number of scales to measure these indigenous social constructs and studied the changes in the personality of Chinese people under societal modernization. His theoretical framework and studies have encouraged other psychologists to study the culture-specific aspects of social relationships and behaviours in Chinese societies. These constructs include *Face, Harmony, Renqing* (reciprocity in relationship), and *Yuan* (pre-destined relationship). Most of these studies and measures are concentrated in the field of social psychology.

In Hong Kong, psychologists have taken on a more cross-cultural perspective to the development indigenous psychology. Many universal as well as indigenously derived constructs are examined in cross-cultural contexts.

In the field of personality assessment, Fanny Cheung and her colleagues have adopted a combined emic-etic approach to develop a personality inventory that includes both universal and culturally salient personality dimensions that make up the personality structure of the Chinese people (Cheung et al., 2001). The Chinese Personality Assessment Inventory (CPAI) provides an example of developing a culturally relevant instrument in a non-Western culture using standard psychological assessment methods in mainstream psychology. They identified a personality factor, *Interpersonal Relatedness*, which could not be encompassed by existing Western personality theories.

According to Cheung and her colleagues (Cheung, Cheung, Wada, & Zhang, 2003), "the goal of indigenous psychology is not only to identify unique aspects of human functioning from the native's perspectives. The identification of culturally relevant dimensions can challenge the encapsulation of mainstream psychology." The original objective in the development of the CPAI was to provide Chinese psychologists with an instrument that captured important dimensions of personality of the Chinese people. The research findings have led the research team down a more theoretical path to examine how the "indigenous" dimensions may also be relevant in other Asian as well as Western cultures. Given the cross-cultural relevance of these dimensions, the CPAI has been renamed the "Cross-cultural Personality Assessment Inventory."

Kwang-Kuo Hwang, Department of Psychology, National Taiwan University, Taipei, Taiwan

Country development and characteristics

Professor Kuo-Shu Yang is the most prominent leader of the movement for the indigenization of psychology in Taiwan, devoting himself to the promotion and organization of the movement since the end of 1970s. He established a Laboratory of Research for Indigenous Psychology in the National Taiwan University, and inaugurated a journal entitled *Indigenous Psychological Research in Chinese Societies* in 1993. As a consequence of his personal inspiration, his students have conducted numerous empirical studies, most of which have been published in local journals using Chinese as their major language (for an English review of those accomplishments, see Yang, 1999).

I finished my Master's thesis under Dr Yang's supervision, and after completing a doctorate, I became a member of the indigenous psychology group in Taiwan. I am strongly opposed to the approach of "naïve positivism," arguing that the mere accumulation of empirical research findings makes little contribution to the progress of social science. In recognition of the fact that the epistemology and methodology of scientific psychology are products of Western civilization, I have insisted that the work of theoretical construction and cultural analysis should be carried out on the basis of Western philosophy of science.

I constructed a theoretical model of Face and Favor on the philosophical basis of scientific realism (Hwang, 1987), intending it to be a formal model that is applicable to various cultures. Using the model as a framework, I analysed the deep structure of Confucianism by the method of structuralism (Hwang, 2001), which enables an understanding of the Confucian cultural heritage from the perspective of social psychology. After that, I analysed the Chinese cultural traditions of Daoism, Legalism, and the Martial school, and published these analyses along with previous works (Hwang, 1995).

My early works are mostly cultural analyses from the perspective of social psychology. They can be used as frameworks for conducting psychological research in Confucian societies, but they do not constitute psychological research in themselves. This approach is unique, and is considered bizarre to most of my colleagues in indigenous psychology. The debates on these issues make our colleagues aware of the divergence and conflicts between various approaches within indigenous psychology. Further debate was stimulated by Yang (1993), who published an article entitled *Why do we need to develop an indigenous Chinese psychology?* and invited several social scientists outside the indigenous camp to comment on his viewpoint, including a historian, an anthropologist, and a philosopher majoring in Western philosophy of science, who questioned the adequacy of his viewpoints from various perspectives.

Recently, I have classified the issues proposed in those debates and analysed them in terms of their standpoint on ontology, epistemology, and methodology (Hwang, 2005). I found that the themes were very similar to those of the debates that have occurred between mainstream and indigenous psychologists in other non-Western countries of the world. I suggested that three levels of breakthroughs must be made in order to ensure progress in indigenous psychology: philosophical reflection; theoretical construction; and empirical research. In order to establish a solid philosophical ground for the future progress of indigenous psychology, I modified the philosophy of constructive realism (Hwang, in press-a), and proposed a conceptual framework to distinguish two types of knowledge, i.e., the scientific knowledge of a microworld constructed by a scientist, and the knowledge used by people in their lifeworlds, which is developed by cultural groups. I then used this framework to explain the modernization of non-Western countries, the emergence of the indigenization movement, the epistemological goal of indigenous psychologies, and the strategy to attain that goal (Hwang, in press-b).

Based on the philosophy of constructive realism, I (Hwang, 2000) have integrated my previous works and have proposed a series of theoretical models on Confucian relationalism. I have used these as frameworks to conduct empirical research on morality (see Hwang, 1998), and conflict resolution in Chinese societies (Hwang, 1997–8). It is expected that this approach might provide a new paradigm for the development of indigenous psychologies in various areas of the world.

Henry Kao, Department of Psychology, Sun Yat-Sen University, Guanzhou, China

Global development and characteristics

There are several sources of influence on the development of global indigenous psychologies: (1) changes in developing countries in the 1970s stimulated endogenous and indigenous rethinking about their social and economic conditions by social and behavioural scientists; (2) their dissatisfaction with what they had learned from Western disciplines for solving problems of their homelands; (3) their growing dissatisfaction with the unquestioned, imitative, and replicative nature of psychological research that is deeply rooted in Western psychology; (4) self-reflection on their own social and cultural characteristics that were beyond Western psychological construction; (5) the awareness by some Western psychologists that the nature of psychology was "monocultural," "Euro-American," and "indigenous psychology of the West"; and (6) the parochial and insular stands of Western psychology, which disregarded the interests and research done in other countries and languages.

Globally, important researchers have been: R. Ardilla, H. Azuma, J. Berry, R. Diaz-Guerrero, D. Ho, H. Triandis, G. Hofstede, C. Y. Chiu, D. Sinha, J. B. P. Sinha, M. H. Bond, V. Enriquez, H. Stevensen, U. Kim, Lagmay, and F. L. K. Hsu.

The most important research questions for indigenous psychologies are to: (1) examine culture-specific patterns of behaviour in developing societies that require new conceptual and theoretical construction beyond that of the Western psychology; (2) identify and develop unique concepts, constructs, and theories; and (3) do research on: brain, language, and cognition; personality and culture; social behaviour and culture; managerial behaviour; and culture, health, and therapies. Research methods suitable for these topics include: archival analysis of classical writings, folk stories, and religious teachings; field experience and participation; surveys, experiments, testing, and clinical observation; conceptual and theoretical development; and cross-cultural comparisons.

Local development

Numerous activities have promoted the development of Chinese indigenous psychology: (1) discussions and conferences on the indigenization of the social and behavioural sciences, which led to the "sinization-of-psychology" movement in Taiwan and Hong Kong from the early l980s; (2) a series of international conferences on Chinese language and cognitive processes was begun in 1981 by the Hong Kong University Department of Psychology; (3) the Conference of Chinese Psychologists, begun in 1995 by the National Taiwan University, has been held regularly in Taipei, Hong Kong, and Beijing; (4) the launch of the journal, *Indigenous Psychological Research in Chinese Societies*, in 1993 by the Department of Psychology, National Taiwan University. These activities have attended to all areas of psychology, including Chinese language, brain and cognition, managerial behaviour, social behaviour, culture-specific concepts, and health and therapeutic interventions.

Among the key researchers involved in these developments are: M. H. Bond, K. S. Yang, C. F. Yang, D. Ho, H. S. Kao, C. Y. Chiu, K. K. Hwang, H. C. Chen, I. M. Liu, C. M. Cheng, F. M. Cheung, L. H. Tan, O. Tzeng.

Local characteristics

Chinese indigenous psychology has focused on a number of themes. These include: (1) research inputs to general understanding and knowledge of human behaviour in order to enrich and complement the contents of contemporary psychology; (2) contributions to theory-building and concept development on the basis of indigenous findings and experiences; (3) contributions to improve the application of psychology to solve problems in developing societies, based on appropriate theories and research conclusions; (4) contributions to inter-cultural communication, understanding, learning, and relations in the context of a globalizing human community.

The salient features of these activities have been: (1) culture-specific and tradition-oriented concept developments and verification; (2) research with universal implications, including work on Chinese language and theory, and on cognitive neuroscience studies, which has contributed to a better understanding of brain functions and the basis of human cognition; (3) research in health and therapy, which has drawn international attention and participation in such areas as acupuncture, Taichi, QiGong, and calligraphy, each with theoretical as well as clinical contributions; and (4) research in social and managerial behaviour that has been valuable for international enterprises operating in the Greater China Circle.

Uichol Kim, and Young-Shin Park, Inha University, Inchon, Korea

Global development and characteristics

Science brings order and understanding into our complex and chaotic world. Physical and biological sciences provided elegant and universal understanding that could be verified and applied to improve the quality of our life. To bring order out of chaos, science proceeds through the process of simplification (hypothesis), generalization (theory), verification (validation), application (testing), and discrimination (refinement). Psychology is one of the last sciences to emerge, attempting to explain the complexities of our inner mind, interpersonal relationship, and socio-cultural realities. During the process of making a science of psychology, we have eliminated central aspects of human functioning (i.e., consciousness, intention, meaning, and goal) in search of abstract and universal laws. Moreover, psychologists hoped to discover universal laws by eliminating the influence of context and culture. As a result, they have eliminated the essence of human being and the validity and generalizability of existing psychological theories have been questioned since the late 1960s (Kim & Berry, 1993).

Indigenous psychologies are necessary since existing psychological theories are not universal and since our perception is influenced by our implicit assumptions, context, and meaning. Existing psychological theories reflect the Euro-American values that champion individualistic, de-contextualized, and analytical knowledge. The second main problem is that the application of psychological knowledge resulted in dismal failures. The limitations of psychological theories came to be recognized by Third World scholars in the early 1970s, who began to question the validity and generalizability of Western psychology. Similar criticisms emerged in Europe, which resulted in the creation of numerous European associations and journals.

Psychologists have tried to discover universal laws of perception by eliminating the subjective aspects, such as meaning and context, and study the perception of physical stimulus, as Ebbinghaus has advocated. However, perception of a physical stimulus is qualitatively different from the perception of a meaningful stimulus.

The three most important theses of indigenous psychologies are: (1) realities appear different because we have different assumptions about how to perceive and interpret our world, (2) perception occurs in context, and (3) we perceive reality using our five senses and using symbols and language developed by our culture.

Country development and characteristics

In East Asia, the need for indigenous psychologies was recognized with the analysis of indigenous concepts, such as the Japanese concept of *amae* ("indulgent dependence"), the Chinese concept of *guanxi* (human relationship), and the Korean concept of *chong* (affectionate attachment for a person, place, or thing). These concepts pointed to the limitation of Western theories that are individualistic. East Asian concepts emphasize human relationship. The Chinese, Japanese, and Korean word for "human being" can be literally translated as "human between." In other words, it is what happens between human beings that make us human. The development of indigenous psychologies that started in the mid-1980s has become an important movement in East Asia.

In Korea, indigenous psychology became synonymous with cultural psychology. In other words, Korean concepts such as *chong*, *chemyon* ("face"), and *han* ("lamentation") have been the focal point of research (Choi, Kim, & Kim, 1997). Recently, indigenous analyses of psychological concepts (e.g., the study of achievement, stress, self, parent–child relationship, school violence, occupational safety, and trust) have been initiated (Kim, 2001). Indigenous psychology is consistent with Albert Bandura's self-efficacy theory (1997), which recognizes human agency, context, and meaning as being central. Both cross-sectional and longitudinal studies yielded results that are highly reliable, valid, and applicable. The development of indigenous psychologies in Korea, East Asia, and around the world promises to provide a psychological understanding of human beings that is truly universal, valid, and applicable.

Kuo-Shu Yang, Graduate Institute of Psychology, Fo Guang University, I Lan, Taiwan

Global development

While indigenous psychologies began with Wilhelm Wundt's 10-volume work on *Völkerpsychologie*, the most recent wave began as local academic movements, mainly in India, the Philippines, Mexico, and Taiwan in the early 1970s. They merged into an international academic movement in the early 1980s through the pioneering and influential writings of Durganand Sinha, Virgilio Enriquez, and Rogelio Diaz-Guerrero. Two collections devoted to indigenous psychologies have been important in promoting them globally (Heelas & Locke, 1981; Kim & Berry, 1993).

The motivation for almost all indigenous psychologies in non-Western countries is reactive and defensive, in the sense that they represent serious attempts to get rid of the global dominance of Western psychology. Most expect that Westernized psychologies will eventually be replaced by indigenous psychologies, each of which represents a culturally based knowledge system for doing a better job of understanding, explaining, and predicting local people's day-to-day behaviour. Most, if not all, indigenous psychologists believe that psychologies in all cultures, Western and non-Western, should be indigenous.

The major purposes of the international academic movement of psychological indigenization are at least fourfold: (1) to point out that Western dominance is unhealthy, not only to the development of meaningful and useful psychologies in non-Western cultures, but also to the construction of a comprehensive, balanced global psychology; (2) to arouse non-Western psychologists' need to develop their own indigenous psychology for their own people; (3) to share each other's experiences in doing indigenous psychological research and in promoting their own indigenous psychologies; and (4) to exchange ideas on how to integrate different indigenous psychologies, Western and non-Western, into a cross-culturally *indigenous* global psychology (Yang, 2000).

While many proponents of indigenous psychology tend to advocate the human science approach (preferring more qualitative methods), I consider both the human science and natural science approaches acceptable when doing indigenous psychological research.

I consider Western psychologists to be indigenous (too numerous to mention here), so I mention only some non-Western indigenous researchers who have made significant contributions internationally: Bor-Shiuang Cheng (Taiwan), Sang-Chin Choi (Korea), Virgilio Enriquez (the Philippines), Rogelio Diaz-Guerrero (Mexico), David Y. F. Ho (Hong Kong), Kwang-Kuo Hwang (Taiwan), Uichol Kim (Korea), Rogelia Pe-Pua (the Philippines), Durganand Sinha (India), Jai B. P. Sinha (India), Susumu Yamaguchi (Japan), Chung-Fang Yang (Hong Kong), Kuo-Shu Yang (Taiwan), and An-Bang Yu (Taiwan).

Local development

I began to feel disillusioned with the Westernized (especially Americanized) Chinese psychology around 1974, mostly because the imported Western concepts, theories, methods, and tools could not do justice to the unique, complicated aspects and patterns of Chinese people's psychological and behavioural functioning. In 1975 I launched an academic movement to indigenize psychological research in Chinese societies (i.e., Taiwan, Hong Kong, and mainland China), and advocated that the Chinese values, ideas, concepts, ways of thinking, and other cultural elements should be reflected as deeply and thoroughly as possible in all phases of psychological research with Chinese participants.

We held an interdisciplinary conference in 1980 in which 60 Chinese scholars from 10 disciplines in the social sciences and humanities from Taiwan, Hong Kong, and Singapore participated. An anthology edited by Yang and Wen and published in Chinese in 1982 has been quite influential in the promotion of the academic movement in Chinese societies.

Starting from 1988, we sped up the tempo to promote indigenous Chinese psychology by: (1) organizing a research team of about 20 professors from different local universities; (2) conducting a set of concerted indigenous empirical studies every 2 or 3 years; (3) holding a large-scale interdisciplinary conference on Chinese psychological functioning every 2 or 3 years; (4) publishing more than 20 books in the Chinese language reporting the methodological, theoretical, and empirical accomplishments of indigenous Chinese psychology; (5) publishing an academic journal entitled *Indigenous Psychological Research in Chinese Societies* (in Chinese) starting from 1993; (6) offering semester courses on indigenous Chinese psychology for graduate and senior undergraduate students in different universities; and (7) offering seminars, workshops, and training programmes on issues concerning indigenous Chinese psychology for graduate students and young faculty members from various universities (for a review, see Yang, 1997).

Ever since 1997, indigenous psychologists in Taiwan have been intentionally increasing their international participation by attending more international conferences and by publishing more papers in international journals and more books with international publishers.

Some indigenous psychologists in Taiwan conducting indigenous research are: Bor-Shiuan Cheng, Ruey-Ling Chu, Li-Li Huang, Kwang-Kuo Hwang, Mei-Chih Li, Tsui-Shan Li, Wen-Ying Lin, LouLu, Chien-Ru Sun, Chung-Kwei Wang, Kuo-Shu Yang, Der-Hui Yee, Kuang-Hui Yeh, and An-Bang Yu.

Global characteristics

There are four global characteristics: (1) most indigenous psychologies are more or less a defensive reaction to the dominance of Western (especially American) psychology in shaping local psychologists' ways of thinking; many indigenous psychologists have experienced difficulty in overcoming resistance, not only from Western psychologists, but also from Westernized local psychologists; (2) their ultimate goal is to create a really indigenous local psychology deeply rooted in the particular historical, cultural, social, and language traditions of their own society; (3) indigenous psychologies are diverse in their favourite topics for study, ways of thinking in conceptualization, favoured methods for data collection, and the types of theories constructed; (4) there are currently more indigenous psychologists endorsing cultural relativism than those endorsing cultural universalism.

Local characteristics

For 50 years, psychology in Taiwan has been under the sole foreign influence of the United States. Most research psychologists in Taiwan have been trained in the States, and Taiwan has had a thoroughly Americanized psychology. However, indigenous psychologists in Taiwan have been determined to refrain from uncritically, or even blindly, applying American psychologists' concepts, theories, methods, and tools to the study of Chinese behaviour. Instead, they have based their studies on Chinese historical, cultural, social, and language traditions, especially the Confucian, Taoist, and Buddhist ones, and have sought to develop an indigenous Chinese psychology suitable for people in all the Chinese societies.

Research, using multiple paradigms, has been completed in more than 40 different areas, including *xiaodao* (filial piety), face behaviour, *yuan* (predestined relational affinity) beliefs, *bao* (reciprocation), *renyuan* (popularity), *yi* (righteousness), *zhongyong* (Confucian Doctrine of the Mean), social-oriented achievement motivation, organizational behaviour, individual traditionality, marital relationship, harmony and conflict, and self psychology (for a review, see Yang, 1999).

Overall, indigenous Chinese psychology is now well received in Taiwan by colleagues who have not adopted such an approach. Indigenous psychologists there have been enjoying equal opportunity in job promotions and research grants.

Elizabeth Protacio-De Castro (formerly Marcelino), Department of Psychology, University of the Philippines, Quezon City, The Philippines, with Melecio C. Fabros, PhD and Reginald Kapunan

Global development and characteristics

The roots of psychology in Asian countries go back two millennia or more in the religio-philosophical treatises and what Ho (1988) calls the "vernacular tradition of the masses," particularly in India, China, and Japan, but also in the Philippines and many other Asian countries.

The indigenized psychologies started to develop globally following the Second World War. This was highlighted as early as 1968, when Campbell labelled modern psychology as a "Euro-American product," and 1974, when Nandy called the imported psychology in the developing world a kind of ready-made intellectual package complete with constructs, concepts, methodology, and instruments for data collection that were far removed from the intellectual traditions and sociocultural realities (Kao & Sinha, 1997). In the last decades Asia has become the major site outside the English-speaking world where cross-cultural research has been making strides.

It should be reiterated (D. Sinha, 1996) that though indigenous psychologies predate cross-cultural psychology, the former in many ways can be considered as an out-growth of the latter in its pursuit of getting mainstream psychology to divest its culture-blind and culture-bound tendencies. The two have enriched each other and should be regarded as complementary. As Kao (1989) has observed, "indigenous psychology based on unique behavioral phenomena must of necessity be the foundation upon which cross-cultural psychology is built."

Western psychology has remained in sharp contrast to religion, but in Eastern thought—especially reflected in the Indian systems of philosophy—religion, philosophy, and psychology do not stand sundered. Likewise, while Western psychology conceptualizes the relationship between man and nature (environment) as dichotomous, in Eastern psychological thinking the two are seen as being in a state of symbiosis.

In the East, psychology has always been intensely practical in its approach. In its effort to be socially relevant, it has developed a perspective that is problem-oriented and interdisciplinary, and is increasingly investigating broader societal issues like deprivation and poverty, social inequality, and agro-economic development. Some important researchers are Durganand Sinha, Virgilio G. Enriquez, Michael H. Bond, D.Y.F. Ho, John Berry, Uichol Kim, Henry S. R. Kao, Anand C. Paranjpe, Kwok Leung, and R. Diaz-Guerrero.

Country development and characteristics

In the Philippines (an American colony for nearly half a century), in the early 1970s there was a strong clamour to dismantle American domination and a call for national self-determination and self-reliance. Filipino social scientists, most of them trained in American universities in the 1950s and '60s, were articulating their dissatisfaction with Western (meaning American) theories and methodologies and the lack of fit between intellectual traditions of less developed countries and Western social science (Atal, 1974). Filipino researchers proclaimed the "limits of Western social research methods in the rural Philippines" (Feliciano, 1965). Most important, the problems caused by the imposition of a foreign language in understanding local culture were recognized.

Upon returning to the Philippines from his doctoral studies at NorthWestern University (Chicago) in 1971, Dr Virgilio G. Enriquez advocated a psychology that truly reflected the Filipino as seen from a Filipino perspective. He, and several of the country's leading social scientists, criticized and corrected earlier (mis)interpretations of supposed national traits by centring on that which truly defines a Filipino: his sense of *pakikipagkapwa* (his "me/other"orientation or shared identity). Furthermore, he challenged the then-existing norm of understanding cultures from the perspective of a dominant culture, and proposed a more democratic "*indigenization from within*" approach towards creating a truly universal psychology.

Enriquez instituted the use of the national language both as the medium of instruction in psychology, and as the perfect entry point in the empirical understanding of the Filipino *diwa* (essence). Enriquez' ideas, together with those of his friends and colleagues (Salazar, Covar, Jocano, and others), succeeded in radicalizing, de-colonizing, rejuvenating, making relevant, and re-inventing psychology in the Philippines.

Enriquez (1985, 1992) defined the major characteristics of *Sikolohiyang Pilipino* (Phillipine psychology). Its philosophical antecedents include (1) empirical philosophy, academic-scientific psychology, the ideas of Ricardo Pascual, and logical analysis of language; (2) rational philosophy, the clerical tradition (Thomistic philosophy and psychology), and phenomenology; and (3) liberalism, the Philippine propaganda movement, the writings of Philippine heroes Jacinto, Mabini, and del Pilar, and ethnic psychology.

Today, some 10 years after his death, his students and followers (e.g., Protacio-Marcelino, Pe-Pua, Guanzon- Lapena, Ortega, Dalisay) have carried on the tradition—expanding on the ideas of Dr Enriquez and refining the theories and methods of *Sikolohiyang Pilipino.*

The same criticisms that were levelled against *Sikolohiyang Pilipino* at its founding are, interesting enough, levelled against it today. Foremost is the issue of who exactly is the "Pilipino" (Salazar, 1991). In a country of multiple ethnicities, this is a valid point. Furthermore, some argue that *Sikolohiyang Pilipino* is still not a discipline as much as a movement. Others claim that it is not logico-positivistic enough, or not critical enough. These criticisms/debates have sustained (and attest to) its continuing popularity.

Leo Marai, Psychology Strand, School of Business Administration, University of Papua New Guinea, Papua New Guinea

Global development

Indigenous psychologies remain as an evolutionary part of a society's psychological way of doing things. However, the systematic presentation of its development was presented by Kim and Berry in 1993 in their edited book entitled: *Indigenous psychologies: Research experiences in cultural context.* In this book, different indigenous psychologists from various countries present their views on the indigenous psychologies that exist, or are emerging in their countries. As reflected from their views, the initiatives came from especially indigenous scholars (usually from Third World countries) who studied in West, but when returning home found that what they had learnt was difficult to apply and, at the extreme, had no relevance. The social developmental problems related to escalating behavioural aspects in developing countries in fact serve as catalysts for developing indigenous psychologies, which may provide some understanding and solutions to these issues. The approach taken is purely indigenous,

defining what is indigenous psychologies and the use of indigenous concepts in understanding psychological process, as well as defining the epistemology underlying indigenous works. A recent article by renowned indigenous psychologist Kim (2001) exemplifies robustly the epistemology and the kind of indigenous psychologies that are truly scientific. Kim principally argues that indigenous psychologies represent a paradigm shift from the positivistic approach that is dominating psychology at present to context, epistemology, and phenomenology in orientation. The important researchers in indigenous psychologies globally include; John Berry (Canada), Uichol Kim (Korea), D. Sinha (India), R. Diaz-Guerrero (Mexico), J. Georgas (Greece), P. Boski (Poland), B. F. Lomov, E. A. Budilova, V. A. Koltsova, and A. M. Medvedev (Russia), F. M. Moghaddam (USA), J. E. Trimble (USA), B. Medicine (USA), V. G. Enriquez (Philippines), R. Ardila (Latin America), D. Jodelet (France), Sang-Chin Choi (Korea), Soo-Hyang Choi (Korea), M. Durojaiye (Africa), Padmal de Silva (Great Britain), D. Yau-Fai Hu (Hong Kong), G. Davidson (Australia), D. Thomas (New Zealand), Samy (Fiji), and Leo Marai (Papua New Guinea).

Country development

Although there was earlier psychological research on indigenous concepts in the area of testing in Papua New Guinea (e.g., Ord, 1972), the first formal call for indigenous psychologies was made by Marai (1997). In his review on the development of psychology in Papua New Guinea, Marai found that psychology has failed in applied and research domains. Such failures were attributed to the influence of Western psychology in local context, which is inappropriate and irrelevant. Marai proposed that the indigenous psychologists should *define* the *appropriate* psychology for the country. Nonetheless, the domination of Western psychology in Papua New Guinea is still evident, especially in the curriculum taught at the universities and in research practices.

Global characteristics

There are three important characteristics of indigenous psychologies globally at present. First, on the theoretical front, various proposals in terms of epistemology and theory has been put forward for indigenous psychologies. An excellent article by Kim (2001) quite vividly demonstrates this trend. He argues for indigenous psychologies to incorporate culture, language, philosophy, and science as products of collective effort, and for the relationship between an individual and a group to be viewed as a dynamic, interactive system of mutual influence. Second, indigenous psychologists who have studied in the West, but return home to find that this kind of psychology is difficult to apply in local context, are the ones contributing to the area of psychological research in the indigenous psychologies arena. That is where the centre of gravity is located and we expect to see a paradigm shift from the mainstream positivistic psychology (for an example, see Kim, 2001). Third, indigenous concepts have contributed to the operationalization of indigenous psychologies in different cultural settings, thus providing scientific validity to its study (Kim & Berry, 1993; Matsumoto, 2001).

Country characteristics

The characteristic of indigenous psychologies in Papua New Guinea (PNG) is the call for *defining* what form of indigenous psychology is relevant for the country (Marai, 1997). Although there is no systematic presentation of indigenous psychology in PNG, what is needed is a follow-up to that call!

Linda Waimarie Nikora, Michelle Levy, Bridgette Masters, and Moana Waitoki, Maori & Psychology Research Unit, University of Waikato, Aotearoa/New Zealand

Global development and characteristics

Indigenous psychology globally is characterized by a reaction against the dominance of the American psychological knowledge "production machine," and the search by indigenous peoples for a voice in their own future. While some indigenous psychologists are in search of psychological universals, some interested in cross-national studies, and some in teasing out minute similarities and differences between cultures, others have bent to the task of solving local challenges within their own contexts with compatible approaches.

Moghaddam (1987) cleverly maps the flow of psychological knowledge, from the First World, in this instance America, to other nations who are considered "importers" rather than exporters of knowledge. Aotearoa/New Zealand (A/NZ) is considered a Second World nation and importer of psychological knowledge, with very little being exported. Omitted in Moghaddam's analysis is the position of Fourth World nations, defined here as indigenous communities positioned within First and Second World nations, for example, Hawai'ians, Aboriginals, and Maori—the original inhabitants of the lands in which they dwell.

The term "indigenous" has two meanings: one refers to these Fourth World peoples, another to all peoples residing in a society; in both, the focus is on peoples who are self-reflecting. The prospect of the Kim and Berry (1993) book made us very excited. This was to be the first time that the interface between "indigenous" and "psychology" would be bought together and explored in such a major and published way. The book was not very satisfying from the perspective of the first meaning of the term. Indeed, what was revealing was the construction of recent migrants as being just as "indigenous" as Maori, Hawai'ian, and Australian Aboriginals! One could not help but feel that the "natives" were being put upon yet again.

Terminology aside, the objectives of an indigenous psychology are agreeable: That is, to develop psychologies that are not imposed or imported; that are influenced by the cultural contexts in which people live; that are developed from within the culture using a variety of methods; and that result in locally relevant psychological knowledge.

Local development

Indigenous psychology in A/NZ has always been a part of how Maori approach wellness, health, and being, stemming from a world-view that values balance, continuity, unity, and purpose. It is not widely written about, yet it is understood and assumed by Maori, and acted upon and expected. Perhaps it is best referred to by the Maori term *tikanga*, or customary practice—those behaviours, values, ways of doing things, and understanding actions that have always and will continue to be with us.

Early social scientists to A/NZ sought, through key informants, to document a Maori view of the world. These writers and, later, Maori academics Buck and Ngata left a hugely rich information base for contemporary psychologists. The search for Maori psychological frameworks often start with early works such as these rather than with PsycAbstracts.

Up until the 1940s, few academic psychologists took an interest in the Maori world. Research through the 1940s to the 1960s was criticized for being "on" Maori, rather than "with" Maori; the work of Beaglehole, Ritchie, and their students in the culture and personality tradition marked an approach to Maori communities and to local contexts that set the background for the development of cross-cultural and community psychology through the 1970s and 1980s (see Ritchie, 1992; Hamerton, Nikora, Robertson, & Thomas, 1992). Although productive, their efforts still stood in the shadow of dominant Western psychological paradigms.

Irrespective of these advances, in 1987, Abbott and Durie (1987) found psychology to be the most monocultural of all the professional training programmes that they surveyed. They argued that to produce graduates able to work effectively with Maori, increased speed towards the inclusion of Maori content in curriculum development needed to occur. Since then, much has been achieved, but still much more needs to be done (Levy, 2002). Perhaps this explains why Maori psychologists and academics have taken their skills and invested their energies in the "Maori development agenda" that has gripped our country for the last two decades.

Most central to advancing the Maori development agenda has been psychiatrist, psychologist, and professor of Maori Studies, Mason Durie (e.g., 1994). Durie's work has become the touchstone for professionals and policy-makers across the health and welfare sectors. He is not only prolific in his ideas, but he also has a clear and concise way of articulating *tikanga*—a necessary skill for any exponent of indigenous psychology in A/NZ.

For psychology, the Maori development agenda is to create psychologies to meet the needs of Maori people in a way that maintains a unique cultural heritage, and makes for a better collective Maori future. It is a journey towards Maori self-determination (Nikora, 2001). Our primary focus has been on the development of a critical mass of indigenous psychologists capable of developing robust *tikanga*-based psychological frameworks. Although a slow process, there is a small yet active group of people who are making a contribution through practice, teaching, research, or involvement in professional organizations (see Nikora, Levy, Masters, Waitoki, Te Awekotuku, & Etheredge, 2003).

T. S. Saraswathi, formerly with the M. S. University of Baroda, Baroda, India

Country development and characteristics

The origin of indigenous psychology in India, as in some other countries in the Orient, is closely entwined with religion. Hinduism, which is described more as a way of life than as a religion, prescribes a code of conduct for human behaviour, recognizing the changing developmental tasks in different life stages.

At the philosophical level, especially in the theory of self-actualization, the states of consciousness are described in great detail and are closely akin to the unconscious, the conscious ego, and the super-ego; transcending these is a super-consciousness or enlightenment. There is also recognition of the base instincts, the emotions (detailed in sculpture, art, music), and the intellect. The self receives particular attention, distinguishing the worldly self, which is bound, from the spiritual self, which can be liberated.

Thus, I see the origins of indigenous psychology in India in Hindu philosophy. Because Hinduism is a way of life, these ideas have permeated the daily life of the population through beliefs, practices, and ethnotheories that continue to influence behaviour in a substantial way.

With respect to the major contributors, I view Prof. Durganand Sinha as having played a lead role, also inspiring the Allahabad school of scholars. Prof. J. B. P. Sinha has also made a distinct contribution, especially in the field of organizational psychology. Others include Prof. R. C. Tripathi, Prof. Girishwar Misra, Prof. Lila Krishnan, and Prof. R. K. Naidu.

In my view, the indigenous psychology perspective does not dominate Indian psychology. There is an increasing and more focused interest; but there is no domination.

The major characteristics of Indian indigenous psychology are not very clear. Perhaps there is an attempt to draw on some of the Indian philosophical concepts that have become an integral part of the Indian psyche (see D. Sinha, 1997).

Jai B. P. Sinha, Assert Institute of Management, Puri, India

Country development and characteristics

Although stray ideas and insights of an indigenous nature appeared in India in the 1950s and 1960s, a clear trend towards the emergence of indigenous psychology was noticed in the 1970s. The trend picked up momentum in the 1980s and subsequently moved towards integrating indigenous and foreign ideas, concepts, and methods. There were at least four factors that played a seminal role:

1. Disenchantment with Western psychology. Indian psychologists replicated Western studies, theories, and methods. An increas-

ingly large number of inconsistent findings and unconfirmed theories compelled them to think afresh.

2. With surging nationalism, there was a trend towards de-colonization of psychological knowledge by searching the philosophical roots of Indian wisdom and retrieving indigenous concepts and psychological processes from the ancient texts.

3. Confronted by the problems of national development and communal conflicts, psychologists found themselves at a loss, because Western psychology did not offer usable solutions or even appropriate perspectives.

4. Formation of the IACCP certainly provided a rallying ground for psychologists from non-Western cultures to think of alternative psychologies. Collaboration with some of the Western psychologists (e.g., John Berry, Harry Triandis, among others) facilitated the process.

As new ideas and approaches from indigenous origins started coming up, Indian psychologists, particularly those who were the front-runners (see D. Sinha, 1997) identified patches of overlap between Indian, Western, and non-Western psychological knowledge, leading to integrative indigenous psychology in India (see J. B. P. Sinha, 2003, for details). A major event that facilitated this process was a series of three sets of surveys of research in psychology, sponsored by the Indian Council of Social Science Research (e.g., Pandey, 1988). The surveys showed the imitative and replicative nature of research, which in turn stimulated many psychologists to conduct innovative studies by drawing ideas from their socio-cultural milieu.

It seems that the Western influence and the ancient Indian psycho-spiritual thoughts filtered through folkways (consisting of common Indian beliefs, preferences, norms, and so on) to generate five overlapping trends towards indigenous psychology in India (J. B. P. Sinha, 2003).

1. A purist endogenous trend supported by beliefs and/or some evidence that the ancient Indian wisdom has patches of similarities with Western psychology. Moreover, it presents a more promising view of psychological well-being (e.g., Bhawuk, 1999).

2. A trend towards endogenous indigenization in which ancient Indian concepts (e.g., *nishakam karma)* are operationalized to show their relevance for the present day (Pande & Naidu, 1992).

3. A purist exogenous trend in which Western concepts and methods (information integration theory and method) are employed to study Indian reality (concept of fairness, group harmony, and so on).

4. A trend towards exogenous indigenization, in which Western concepts (such as ingratiation, achievement motivation, etc.), framework (e.g., psycho-analytic, Kakar, 1978), and methods (for example, level of aspirations, field dependence) were modified and adapted to examine Indian reality.

5. A trend towards an integrative indigenization, in which Western and Indian concepts and methods were integrated to produce hybrid concepts and theories (e.g., nurturing task leadership, J. B. P. Sinha, 1995).

In the future, all five trends are going to get stronger, creating a multi-corned space for building indigenous psychology in India that might contribute to a more enriched universal psychology. However, indigenous psychology is still a "little culture" dominated by Western psychology.

Fathali M. Moghaddam, Department of Psychology, Georgetown University, Washington, DC, USA

Global development

Indigenous psychology in non-Western societies evolved as a result of two sets of influences, internal and external to non-Western societies. The internal influences concerned resources, and particularly reaching a critical mass of trained psychologists.

This growth in internal resources coincided with a number of movements internationally. First, through the United Nations Development Programme (UNDP) and various UN agencies, non-Western psychologists came across the concept of "appropriate technology," and soon learned to raise the question of "appropriateness" with respect to imported psychological knowledge (Moghaddam & Taylor, 1986). Second, in the 1960s a number of European psychologists, for example, Henri Tajfel and Serge Moscovici in social psychology, were spearheading a movement to establish a distinct European psychology, separate from the dominant United States model (Moghaddam, 1987). These developments influenced Asian and African psychologists to do the same, as is apparent from their new journals. A third factor acting as an impetus for indigenous psychology in non-Western societies has been minority movements in the West: feminist psychology, Black psychology, and Latino psychology.

Country development

Without doubt the most important event leading to a movement toward indigenous psychology in Iran is the revolution of 1978. The Shah was viewed as a puppet of the West and particularly the United States, a roadblock to any attempt to achieve an authentic Iranian voice, including one in psychology. The attack on the Shah was associated with an attack on Western world-views, particularly in psychology and economics. When the universities re-opened after the fall of the Shah's regime in the "spring of revolution" in 1979, there was tremendous pressure on psychologists to abandon traditional Western models and develop an alternative psychological science, one "appropriate" for the Iranian population (Moghaddam, 2002). The criticisms ranged from the characteristics of research methods used in traditional Western psychology, to the assumptions underlying the very foundations of Western psychology. However, the last quarter of a century have shown that the development of an indigenous psychology is not an easy path to follow, particularly under difficult political conditions.

The movement toward an indigenous psychology in Iran has been confronted by major challenges arising from the post-revolution political context. The so-called "cultural revolution" of the early 1980s in Iran, in important ways resulted in even greater reliance on US psychology. A review of the main texts, journals, research projects, and conferences in Iran reveals that although there is still genuine interest in developing an indigenous psychology, the reliance on Western and particularly US models continues to be considerable. This is particularly true in the most competitive universities, where professors with the highest status are those with the greatest success in working with traditional Western models of psychology.

Global characteristics

There are three major international trends to be considered:

1. Increased international trade and communications; associated with this is increased export of traditional US psychology to different parts of the world.

2. Serious and, to some extent, successful attempts by non-Western psychologists to move toward indigenous psychology using alternative methods and models, particularly in parts of South America, the Indian subcontinent, mainland China, and South Korea. These indigenization movements are particularly associated with new qualitative/discursive methods, and a rejection of the traditional causal model of behaviour.

3. Some progressive movements to develop indigenous psychology in Russia and former Soviet block countries, based on Vygotsky and others, rather than on orthodox Marxist-Leninist ideology. The re-discovery of Vygotsky is revitalizing indigenous psychology in Russia and elsewhere (Moghaddam, 2002).

Country characteristics

Indigenous psychology in Iran currently involves at least three different movements. A movement (1) to develop an "Islamic psychology" was present in major universities from at least the early 1970s and continues to produce intriguing monographs (in Farsi). However, probably because of its ideological leanings and lack of attention to empirical research, this "Islamic psychology" is receiving more attention in schools of theology and philosophy than in the more prominent departments of psychology.

Whereas the movement towards "Islamic psychology" is sanctioned by the Iranian authorities, efforts to develop an indigenous psychology of (2) gender and of (3) democracy and social change (Moghaddam, 2002) have not been actively supported, and are often seen as being associated with movements opposed to the Islamic government. However, because in some major universities over 85% of psychology students are female, and because of the continuing political struggles in Iran, it is inevitable that at least some Iranian psychologists should seek to develop a psychological science that more effectively addresses the issues of gender and democracy in Iran. This struggle has led to a paradoxical situation: In many cases censors are permitting the translation and publication of traditional US texts in Iran, but not allowing the publication of feminist and liberation psychology by Iranian authors. This is because in many ways traditional US texts are conservative and non-threatening, relative to feminist and liberation psychology.

A. Bame Nsamenang, Centre de ressources pour le développement humain, Université de Yaoundé, Yaoundé, Cameroon

Global development

Every cultural community the world over has an indigenous psychology, whether articulated or not. Thus, human psychological functioning predates psychology as an academic discipline. Why is there a gulf between academic psychology and the one that is accumulating as indigenous psychology? It is clear that extant psychological knowledge has been wrung from predominantly one group of human beings, not from a representative sample of humanity. Can psychological research be carried out on all human beings? Is psychology's subject matter, the human being, a global species? A search for answers to these rogue questions can begin to locate the conceptual origin of indigenous psychology at a point in human history when, wittingly or unwittingly, one group of human beings considered itself to be more human than all the others. This then led to efforts to exclude the behaviour and developmental paths of "outlandish" humans from a discipline that studied "true humanity." For example, while all other peoples had culture, civilization was "something that belonged to Europe as a treasure that shall be enjoyed by the entire planet" (Mignolo, 1998, p. 33). Thus, somewhere about European Enlightenment, the academic disciplines emerged and these efforts transformed into the distinction between the civilized and savage minds; and eventually down to our day into mainstream psychology and other psychologies, including indigenous psychology.

Psychology can thus be regarded as an outreach discipline of Europe's civilizing mission, or more accurately as its civilizational studies. Efforts to distinguish psychology from indigenous psychology reinforce this point and are better interpreted as attempts to clarify the "foundation of a field of study that located Europe as locus of enunciation and other civilizations of the planet as the locus of the enunciated" (Mignolo, 1998, p. 33). Mignolo further refers to "the connivance between disciplinary foundations and colonial powers" (p. 34). Today, mainstream psychology and Western forces of globalization sustain the connivance.

Psychology is much more an intellectual arm of Europe's civilizing mission and much less a universal science of human behaviour. One image of psychology is as a technological gadget that improves in historical time with Western civilization and scientific progress; hence the distinction between technological and nontechnological intelligences (Mundy-Castle, 1974)—respectively, of psychology and indigenous psychology. One evidence of this in publication traditions is that the sources of data from non-European research participants have to be unambiguously explicated, which is not typically the case with data from Europe and the "mainstream" population in its first class diaspora, North America.

Although the conceptual origin of indigenous psychology is much earlier, a reading of the export and import of psychological concepts and methods is replete with reactions to efforts to "indigenize" or culturize them to the US marketplace and US psychology, which is itself an indigenous psychology. Publications by D. Sinha (1997) for India, and for Africa by Durojaiye (1993) and Nsamenang (2001), highlight the origins of indigenous efforts to understand local behaviour or the rise of reaction against the hegemony of an imported (imposed) psychology, whether from the US or elsewhere.

Local development

The efforts to "domesticate" psychological knowledge in Cameroon, as elsewhere in Africa, are linked to resistance against the imposition of colonial knowledge systems, which began centuries ago and continue today in various forms. Psychology is a very young and fledgling discipline in Cameroon, and is still largely tied to the apron strings of service disciplines like education, social work, and medicine (Nsamenang, 1993, 1995). Accordingly, the history of the development of indigenized psychology in Cameroon, as in much of the continent, begins with efforts to appropriate these disciplines and/or services to national realities. Two examples of academic efforts are Nsamenang's (1992) publication of *Human Development in Cultural Context: A Third World Perspective* and a workshop on Child Development and National Development held in Yaounde, Cameroon in 1992 (Nsamenang & Dasen, 1993).

Global characteristics

First, with the increasing salience of psychological phenomena, local precepts and the voices of research participants increasingly find their entry into psychological science. Second, indigenous psychology has sensitized an otherwise insensitive psychological community to the diversity of its subject matter. Third, in spite of resistance to the conceptualization of the diversity of the discipline's subject matter, growing numbers of psychologists are becoming aware that some concepts and methods are not applicable to the global human condition. This is leading to an expansion of visions and efforts to evolve new methods that capture hitherto excluded psychological phenomena. The so-called "soft" methods of qualitative research (Serpell & Akkari, 2001) fall within these new efforts. Fourth, the most "resistant cohort" of psychologists are further splintering the discipline and focusing their splinters more in biology than on culture, given that biology is more amenable to new technologies.

Local characteristics

Efforts to indigenize psychology in Cameroon are inchoate. However, two trends are noticeable. First, efforts are being made to free education/training curricula from excessive Eurocentrism and to indigenize the training of professionals and scholars (Ministry of Education, 1995), including psychologists. Second, developmental research is endeavouring to focus on African social ontogeny, a developmental path in life-span perspective within an African world-view, espoused by Nsamenang (1992, 2001).

Carl Martin Allwood, Department of Psychology, Lund University, Lund, Sweden

Global development and characteristics

Human understanding is dependent on the social and cultural conditions in which it is generated and sustained. Indigenized psychologies exemplify what may happen to a scientific knowledge tradition developed in one cultural context (the West) when it is moved to other cultural contexts (Allwood, 1998). By indigenized psychologies I mean psychologies that are developed as a reaction to mainstream psychology as it has been, and is, developed mainly in the USA. I exclude from this definition the indigenous psychologies that have traditionally been part of many cultures (see Allwood, 2002).

The history of the indigenized psychologies is in large part specific to each country or cultural region. Researchers in different societies have reacted to Western psychology from their own conditions. Generally, there appear to be two motives for the development of the indigenized psychologies, one practical and one cultural/ideological.

The practical motive is that in many non-Western contexts Western psychology has often been found not to be very useful for solving social problems. The cultural/ideological motive is that in many non-Western countries Western psychology is considered not to reflect the researcher's own cultural conceptions or understandings. For example, one may miss perspectives, theoretical understandings, or concepts from one's own culture. Moreover, Western psychology is often felt to be too liberal, individualistic, or materialistic. The desire to indigenize one's own psychological research can be seen as an effect of a broader post-colonial reaction. In many countries, Western psychology was introduced during the colonial period and the indigenization process has often been part of a more general national post-colonial reaction (D. Sinha, 1997).

Different aspects of Western psychology have been indigenized. These include *researching phenomena and populations from one's own country or culture*, but still using problems and methods from Western psychology. A more ambitious form is to focus on *problems that come out of the needs of the country's own culture and society*. Another approach is to indigenize the *research methodology* in order to make it more appropriate to one's own research context. One can also attempt to use or *develop concepts and theories* that are more representative of one's own cultural tradition. Finally, *specific ontological postulates* may be introduced (e.g., Ghamari-Tabrizi, 1996, and other articles in the same issue).

Globally, it is important to emphasize the heterogeneity of indigenized psychologies since they are a product of their own specific social and cultural conditions. However, shared features among various indigenized psychologies present an interesting empirical research question. As described above, a common denominator is to object to US American psychology. Similarly, the role played by international conferences and associations in the development of the indigenized psychologies deserves further research.

Local development and characteristics

At the beginning of the 20th century, the early development of the field of psychology in Sweden was influenced by various continental European traditions (for a brief overview, see Lundberg, 2001). However, after the Second World War, Sweden was heavily influenced by Anglo-American culture, and continental philosophical approaches became less popular in psychology. Swedish researchers in psychology oriented themselves mainly to US and British psychology. The same is the case today. There is no noticeable tendency to develop a specifically Swedish psychology, except possibly in the few examples described below. However, different types of measurement scales developed in the US and Britain are translated into Swedish and standardized in the Swedish setting. And in applied contexts, there is a felt need to investigate phenomena as they occur in Sweden.

In social psychology, there is some interest in European aspects such as the work of Henry Tajfel on social identity. Some parts of clinical psychology have been influenced by psychoanalysis (including, in highbrow academia, Lacan) and its dynamic offspring. There is also interest among some researchers (for example in organizational psychology) in the ongoing development of the ex-Soviet social cultural school of Vygotsky and Leontiev. Given these few exceptions, there is very little contact between Swedish psychology and the more country-specific psychologies of countries outside of the Anglo-American cultural sphere.

A rare instance of a more typically Swedish psychology is the "psychology of labour," which was influenced by the reformist social democratic ideas that have dominated the political scene and the administration of Sweden in the last 70 years. It has been oriented towards improving conditions for employees both in state-run organizations and services and in private companies. This field of psychology was *one* influence behind the development of the Scandinavian Systems Development School and its approach to the development of computer systems, which emphasizes the importance of the role of employees in the development and introduction of new computer systems in the workplace (see Allwood & Hakken, 2001).

John Berry, Department of Psychology, Queen's University, Kingston, Canada

Global development and characteristics

Much of the interest in indigenous perspectives in psychology has been in societies commonly called "developing." Often overlooked is the idea that WASP (Western Academic Scientific Psychology) is itself an indigenous psychology rooted in a particular cultural tradition. Moscovici (1972) argued that the social psychology then in existence was a set of topics and findings that were rooted in the interests and social problems of one society (the USA). He called upon European social psychologists to examine their own social reality, and to develop their own concepts, and research

findings based on their own reality. At the same time, Berry and Wilde (1972) published a book that promoted the idea that Canadian social psychology was characterized by imitative (of USA) research, but could (or should) be rooted in some core features of Canadian society. These core features might be issues of: living in the North; understanding both English–French, and Aboriginal–non-Aboriginal relations; and researching multiculturalism, so that this social reality could succeed as a viable way of living together in culturally plural societies. While the European initiative took root, and led to the establishment of an association and a journal, the Canadian initiative was greeted as a virtual absurdity!

At much the same time, indigenous psychologies were being developed in many societies, but were not really coordinated into a new world view about the nature of the discipline. However, those who were becoming aware of the international spread of the approach also proposed that there could be a comparative (rather than only a local) use of the emerging concepts and data. Proposals were made for "cross-indigenous" or "universal" approaches that would integrate the emerging ideas and findings from many societies. One attempt to bring many of these approaches together was made in a book edited by Kim and Berry (1993).

Country development and characteristics

As noted above, initial proposals were made in the early 1970s to develop a psychology that would be more relevant to understanding behaviour rooted in the contextual realities of Canada. These proposals were accompanied by an explicit rejection of the automatic relevance and validity of psychology developed elsewhere. For example, Berry (1974) likened psychology as a science to a blueprint of a machine or house, and asked: If our blueprint was created elsewhere, for a different reality, how can we hope to make sense of the complex reality that we have before us? I went on to suggest that we should begin to create a new blueprint, one that considers the core features of our own society, and then launch a programme of conceptualization and research that corresponds to it. This proposal shares much of the thinking that was underway elsewhere in the indigenization movement. However, in Canada it coincided with a form of emergent nationalism, and we were criticized as being "anti-American" and overtly nationalist, rather than seeking a more relevant discipline. (Note that being "non-American" in

Canada is often assumed to be the same as being "anti-American"!) Some psychologists in Canada participated in this initiative, but most did not, believing it (possibly quite rightly) to be a barrier to their career advancement.

Subsequent work focused on the distinction between psychology *in* Canada, and a psychology *of* Canada (Berry, 1983). The former was an imported version of the discipline, usually without modification, and resembled the "imposed etic" variety of work more generally seen in cross-cultural psychology. The latter is an indigenous or "societal" psychology that takes the local context as its starting point, and resembles the "emic" perspective. To develop this, I proposed a matrix that identified three special features of Canadian society that should inform the development of a Canadian psychology: (1) our "northern" ecosystem, with a particular focus on its primary inhabitants (indigenous peoples), and those that move there (migrant and seasonal workers, miners, hunters, trappers, etc.); (2) our "dualism," based on the substantial representation in our population of people from France and Great Britain (involving the use of two languages, bilingualism, intercultural relations and conflict, etc.); and (3) our "pluralism," based on the increasing range of cultural origins and diversity of our population (involving studies of immigration/refugee phenomena, inter-ethnic attitudes, policy orientations, and changing institutions). These three sets of phenomena all involve a process of mutual acculturation, an area of particular interest to me and many other psychologists in Canada. The second dimension of this matrix was a set of four psychological domains: (1) social, (2) clinical, (3) educational, and (4) work psychology. Considerable work had already been accomplished in the areas of bilingualism (by W. E. Lambert and his colleagues) and with indigenous peoples (mainly by anthropologists), but most of the rest of the work proposed in the matrix remains to be done.

Pawel Boski, Warsaw School of Social Psychology, Warsaw, Poland

Global development and characteristics

In this contribution, the concepts "cultural psychology" and "indigenous psychology" are used as equivalent (C/IP for convenience). C/IP is different from cross-cultural psychology (C-CP) in terms of the role and amount of culture they postulate for psychology (Boski, 2002).

C/IP studies the human psyche as embedded in the web of meanings and symbols or mediated by artefacts. It is contrasted with mainstream psychology by the following three criteria: (1) making a sharp distinction between humans and animal species, (2) postulating *cultural psyche* rather than *pure* thoughts, feelings, etc. This second criterion is also the source of differentiation between C-CP and C/IP, (3) seeing psyche as intrinsically formed (or shaped) by culture, i.e., culture is not seen as a quasi-independent variable of which individuals can become stripped or "unpacked," as C-CP wants it.

Thus, the following is a framework for a discipline that constitutes itself in opposition, or as complementary, to mainstream psychology and to cross-cultural psychology: *The study of the mediation of psychological processes by cultural artifacts (tools, symbols, scripts, normative constraints, philosophies, archetypes, etc.), which create the context and sense of meaning and intention, instead of studying pure psychological processes in abstract and in articifial experiments. Since cultural contextual mediation is always specific, cultural psychology must be indigenous psychology, by definition.*

C/IP was originally initiated by non-Western authors dissatisfied with C-CP's universalist paradigms and approaches. Today, when a standard C-CP study becomes a multinational investigation, C/IP has the ambition of complementing *globalization* with *localization*.

The literature on C/IP can be separated into: (1) conceptual-programmatic works postulating and drawing attention to the need for C/IP (D. Sinha, 1997; Kim, 2001; and many contributors in Kim & Berry, 1993); (2) research-based theoretical contributions. Examples of C/IP psychologists are: Cole (1996), Wierzbicka (1999), Nisbett (2003), and Kitayama and Markus (2000); this author identifies himself with the latter group.

C/IP projects can be quite specific (ethnic) or present grand schemes rooted in core elements of civilizations. Usually, indigenous constructs are language-specific and remain basically not translatable into other languages (i.e., *lost in translation*), e.g.: *amae* (Japanese), *lajya* (Hindi), *cheong/simcheong* (Korean), *sarmatism* (Polish), *simpatico* (Latin/Mexican). According to this author's view, the most adequate way of presenting indigenous concepts to foreigners (including cultural psychologists!) is through pictorial means and not through verbal code, where the phenomenon of *lost in translation* will most likely occur.

Today's main impetus for cultural psychology clearly comes from American-East Asian comparative studies, conducted by Markus and Kitayama, Nisbett, Kaiping Peng, and their associates. These studies are concerned respectively with cultural constructions of independent-interdependent self, and analytical-holistic modes of thinking. While comparative in methodology, these authors' projects are clearly distinct from mega-projects based on samples from all over the world. It is also hard to miss the fact that researchers from these camps do not participate in IACCP activities.

Chinese, Japanese, Korean, and other cultures of East Asia have the richness of the past and the dynamism of today, which must result in truly indigenous formulations vis-à-vis Western psychology. Kim and Yang (in press) exemplifies this trend.

Europe is currently undergoing tremendous cultural changes, two of which appear most crucial: (1) massive immigration from materially poor regions of the world; and (2) integration of 30 nation states into the EU, after many years of being ravaged by wars. These processes are of such magnitude that the existing frameworks of acculturation (between two cultures) are not sufficient here. It may become less and less productive to postulate indigenous psychologies based on fixed ethnic entities. Rather we can expect developments towards a truly multicultural and multilayered world, marked by a growing post-modernist *zeitgeist*, and personalized cultures. What I am envisaging here is a world in which the equation indigenous = ethnic (folk) psychology will be marginalized.

Country development and characteristics

Indigenous psychology can refer to problems specific both to a given society and to cultural values. Two examples of work in Polish indigenous psychology are Boski (1993) and Wierzbicka (1999).

In Poland, humanist concerns are one leading theme (Boski, 1993, in press). *Humanism* is conceived as care for other people, involvement in close, affective relations with them, and prosocial concern for their well-being; it is contrasted with materialist consumerism and business orientation.

Wierzbicka is a psycho-semanticist and a critic of Ekman's approach to the cross-cultural study of emotions. She employs the concept of *cultural script* and investigates emotional expressions embedded in such scripts as they occur in works of literature and personal documents (memoirs) (e.g., Wierzbicka, 1999).

The construct of cultural script is methodologically essential for Wierzbicka's and my own

studies (see Boski, Van de Vijver, Hurme, & Miluska, 1999). It is operationalized by the type of research materials used: pictures, videos, feature films, pieces of literature, etc. This enables us to study cultural perception-evaluation-identification in a single culture or comparatively. In contrast, studies conducted by C-CP are preoccupied with a cultural "stimulus equivalence." We advocate just the opposite: The more of culture in research material, the better.

DISCUSSION

The indigenous psychologies represent attempts by researchers in many countries to develop psychologies that are rooted in their own culture's understanding of human behaviour. Since the new indigenous psychologies (IPs) can be seen as an important addition to Western psychology (WP), we invited prominent scholars with an interest in IP, from all over the world, to give short statements of their views on the development and characteristics of IP. Our analysis of the 15 responses (including our own) revealed 8 important themes. These themes were the ones most frequently discussed, and reveal a set of views that were often, but not always, fairly consensual about the development and character of IP across the various societies sampled. In this Discussion, we provide some comments on these themes, and link them to similar issues that have appeared in the recent literature on IP. The first theme discussed below concerns the origins and development of the IPs. The subsequent themes cover different aspects of the character of IPs: their aim to be based on and investigate cultural roots and issues, IPs as a reaction to WP, IPs' view of appropriate methods, and their relation to WP and to other versions of culture-oriented psychology. Next, some of the contributors' hopes for a more universally valid psychology based on the results of the IPs are discussed. In the last theme we discuss the extent to which the IPs can be seen as homogeneous or heterogeneous.

Origins and development of IP

When writing about the origins and development of the IPs, the contributors distinguished different stages in their development. A first stage recognized by many was the traditional, ancient teachings by philosophers and religious teachers in their own culture. However, it was usually recognized that the modern IPs, although drawing on these teachings, are distinct from them.

There are two important factors behind the development of the new IPs. First, post-colonial, often anti-Western, reactions involved a critical attitude towards intellectual influences from the West, including the imported WP. Second, and in line with the first, observations that the imported WP was not useful for solving local social problems were conducive to the development of IPs. Other sources of inspiration for the development of some IPs were early European attempts by Moscovici and others to form a specifically European social psychology. The deliberate activities of specific individual researchers were reported to have been important, often from the 1970s onwards, for the development of some IPs. Examples are Kuo-Shu Yang for Taiwan and the Chinese societies, Virgilio Enriquez for the Philippines, and Durganand Sinha for India. At the same time, John Berry and colleagues initiated a movement towards a Canadian IP. These researchers (and others), together with published books, including edited anthologies (e.g., Kim & Berry, 1993), then inspired younger scholars who were experiencing some difficulties in applying WP to problems in their own country, to start the development of IPs. In addition, other books and journals, and proceedings of international conferences (such as those initiated by Yang, and the IACCP and IAAP), were reported by some to have facilitated the development of IPs. Thus, both local and international events were important, especially for later initiatives, to develop IPs. Finally, indigenous developments of psychology may be present in a country even when there is no approach to psychology present that identifies itself as an IP and when the development has presumably not been much affected by post-colonial reactions or by the development of the IPs in other countries. Sweden exemplifies such a country and it is of relevance that political ideologies have still influenced the few indigenous approaches to psychology that exist in that country.

Characteristics of IP

We next discuss various aspects that characterize the IPs. This theme was attended to by all the contributors and relates to the aim of IPs to be based on and to investigate cultural roots and issues. IP was seen as an attempt to produce a local psychology within a specific cultural context. By "cultural," we mean here a set of background features within which a group of people has developed over the course of their history, including a set of institutions (social, political, economic, religious) and a shared set of meanings and values. The local culture is unanimously identified both as a source of inspiration for developing an IP, and as a concrete goal in achieving an IP. As a source, these cultural contexts provide various inputs, including a group's language, philosophical and ethical frameworks, sacred beliefs, and social structural arrangements. As a goal, cultural meanings give shape to the emerging IP, including the concepts adopted, the methods used, and the interpretive frames of reference that pattern the final product. Their unanimous concern with this theme means that it is widely accepted both as a local characteristic and as a global one.

IP as a reaction against WP

The next theme, which was discussed by nearly all the contributors, concerns IP as a reaction to the dominance of WP. The contributions show that IP is a reaction by scholars and practitioners to the dominance of WP. For many respondents, both the impetus to develop IP and its specific character are "reactive." IP is viewed as a response that rejects the validity and usefulness of WP in their societies. This negative aspect is accompanied by a positive one: IP also seeks to provide an alternative psychology to the massive presence of WP in their own society, and internationally. It is asserted that WP has been "exported" by Western psychologists, through their powerful array of associations, research grants, fellowships, journals, and textbooks. But it is also recognized that WP has been "imported" by those who have received advanced education in the West, and who continue to attempt to practise WP in their own countries (once called "Yankee doodling" by some scholars from India). For some, the rejection of WP is rooted in their recognition that WP is "culture-bound" and not universal, and is really only one of many possible IPs; it may be valid and useful in the West (like other IPs for their societies), but it is rejected as being ethnocentric—even as a form of scientific colonization when imposed on others. This failure of WP is expressed as giving rise to concerns and dissatisfaction, or even as *dismal*. Here are mentioned Western disciplines, theories, and tools as well as WP theories and perspectives. In addition, IPs are sometimes described as being more concretely oriented: According to one contributor, Eastern IPs are "intensely practical." This emphasis on application and practicality is linked to the frequent role of psychology in educational, clinical, and developmental activities in many societies, both within different levels of university education and in governmental programmes. For a few, dissatisfaction with WP has resulted in a number of distancing actions, including not publishing in WP journals and not presenting their findings in the English language (although there were also other important reasons for presenting their findings in their home language). This strategy seems to have been pursued to allow them to draw back from the dominant influence of WP, and to give themselves cultural space within which to rethink their research and teaching careers, and to develop their own IP.

Appropriate methods for IP

The next theme, covered by nearly all the contributors, relates to the contributors' discussion of appropriate methods for the IPs. There was a general consensus that WP methods are not universal and should not be used uncritically. Most of the contributors stated that it is important for IP that the research methods used are appropriate to their cultural and social context. In this way issues and phenomena not explored in WP might be more successfully explored. However, there was quite a range of views about what methods are legitimate in an IP context and quite a range of methods were mentioned; some contributors, indeed, noted that IPs use "multiple paradigms." Quite a few contributors felt that nonpositivistic methods, methods from human science (ranging from archival studies of ancient texts to phenomenology), or so-called "qualitative methods" were appropriate for IP. However, some contributors argued that IP might well use natural science approaches such as experiments, use Western concepts and methods, or do studies from the point of view of Western philosophy of science. Other examples of methods approved of are cross-sectional studies, longitudinal studies, comparative studies (e.g., "rooted in core elements of civilizations," or cross-cultural), field experience or participation, testing, and clinical observations. The importance of investigating psychological phenomena by means of the local language and of using samples of genuine local cultural material (including video recordings, or vignettes in questionnaires) was pointed out.

Theory in IP

All the contributors discussed theory building in the IPs and sometimes contrasted it with that in WP or (less often) related IP to cultural psychology

and cross-cultural psychology (C-CP). WP was usually viewed as an indigenous psychology, and since WP is not universal it was argued that it should not be applied blindly. The style of theorizing in IP, in contrast to WP theorizing, was felt by many to be to build theories on the basis of local phenomena, findings, and experiences (i.e., bottom-up). According to some contributors it is typical for IP, in contrast to WP, to focus on phenomena such as consciousness, meaning, intention, and goals, viewing these as formed by the cultural and social context. Some contributors asserted that the IPs differ from WP in that they are nonanalytic and nonindividualistic, in the sense that they do not separate human beings from nature, or religion from philosophy and psychology. Due to the differences between IPs and WP, influences from IPs were seen as being able to open up, invigorate, and to improve WP. Different contributors argued both that the IPs are critical of the foundations of WP, and that IPs sometimes have "patches" of similarity to WP and sometimes can integrate WP and IP concepts or use WP concepts to study local phenomena. In addition, there were different views concerning the relation between the IPs on the one hand, and cultural psychology and cross-cultural psychology on the other. Some contributors saw the IPs as a kind of cultural psychology, being close to or even identical with the socio-historical school of Vygotsky and the activity theoretical tradition of Leontiev, or to some kinds of social anthropology, and separate from cross-cultural psychology. However, the view that IP and cross-cultural psychology have an interactive relation, enriching one another, was also represented.

Reactions to IP

As a movement inspired by local cultural concerns, and as a reaction to the dominance of WP, it is no surprise that nearly half of the contributors emphasized the reaction to their work on IP. Critical reaction came from various sources, including colleagues, university administrations, and national associations. It is easy to understand that in an academic environment, where progress in one's career often depends on "international" publishing and the teaching of WP (using textbooks and journals), turning one's back on WP can be threatening to a person's own advancement. It is less easy to understand why the pursuit of IP would be so threatening to others. One possibility is that (as for culture-oriented psychology in general) the implicit message of IP is that the psychology (WP) being used and taught by others is not valid. IP essentially says to colleagues: "You do not know what you think you know about human behaviour," at least not until you know it in context, both locally and comparatively. It may also be that arguing for the relevance of other cultures' understanding in the formation of psychology is experienced as introducing relativism and irrelevant concerns. However, the recent rise of the IP movement has given the IPs some legitimacy for the view that people should be understood in terms of their own cultures, rather than always in terms of some foreign culture. It has also provided some protection against charges of parochialism and nationalism, but earlier the difficulties were evident. At the same time it is encouraging that some contributors felt that in their own country there had been no such discrimination against IP. In addition, it is also interesting to note that in at least one contribution (concerning Iran) some forms of IPs were politically supported, whereas other forms were politically disapproved!

IP as a contribution toward universal psychology

Somewhat more than half of the contributors discussed the possibilities of developing a more universal psychology via a comparative integration of the different IPs. One of the pioneers of IP (Enriquez, 1993) argued that by comparing IPs from different societies (the "cross-indigenous method") we might observe an "overall pattern" of human behavioural development and expression. Similarly, Berry and Kim (1993) argued that the comparative method could be used to discern what may be common or "universal" about human behaviour. For both, only when many IPs are available will we be able to achieve a truly pan-human psychology. In keeping with these observations, the contributors who discussed this theme emphasized the need to achieve such a broader picture, arguing that the science has a dual responsibility: to understand people in their own terms (IP), and to search for general principles of human behaviour. The development of an IP is valuable in its own right, but they may also collectively serve as building blocks in creating a more general psychology. If the use of the comparative method actually achieves such a global psychology, it could serve as a challenge to the presumed universal status of WP. In other terms, WP was seen as an "imposed etic," IPs as "emic," and the more general outcome of the comparative enterprise was argued to be to create a "derived etic" psychology that would stand in clear contrast with current WP. However, it may be noted that while the "derived etic psychology" may be more informed by many other cultures, it would still remain anchored in one specific cultural understanding.

Variations in views of IP

In most of the themes above we have discussed the contributors' views on various aspects of the IPs; in many of these themes we found that the contributors agreed fairly well. For example, all the contributors reacted to the dominance of WP (although the target for this criticism varied from *Western* to the *USA* to *Europe*), and saw IP as a kind of psychology that aims to base psychology on the local societal/cultural features of the researcher's home base. Likewise, the contributors agreed on the need to have IPs in their own societies in order to improve psychology's usefulness in solving social problems. However, there were also many signs of different views and approaches prevalent among the IPs and among the contributors. In this final theme we discuss the degree of homogeneity or heterogeneity of the IPs.

A common denominator for the IPs appears to be an interest in researching indigenous concepts and phenomena, but some of the contributors also expressed an interest in investigating local forms of concepts deriving from WP. With respect to methods there was not much sign of homogeneity between the IPs, but if anything, methods influenced by human science appeared to be well accepted. The contributors handled the role of religion in IP in different ways. Some Asian contributors mentioned religious influences on the IP. As examples: Philippine IP was described as being influenced by Catholic philosophy and as not separated from religion and philosophy; Indian IP was described as being based on Hindu philosophy; and in Iran, at least some versions of IP are clearly influenced by, or even based on, Islam. Other IPs, for example Canadian, do not appear to be very influenced by religion at all.

In brief, these observations illustrate that the cultural climate of the country influences the specific IP. They also show the diversity of the IPs. Similarly, the fact that some contributors reported that a number of different approaches to IP have developed in their country invites the same conclusion. For example, the situation in Iran, with an Islamic-oriented IP and other IPs working with gender and democracy issues, is a case in point. India appears to be another example. Here, five "overlapping trends towards IP in India" were described. Church and Katigbak (2002), in an overview of IP in the Philippines, described many different approaches to the IP. Whether it is most appropriate to speak of *one* or *many* IPs, even within one society, appears to be an open question. In contrast to such fragmentation of IPs, it is of interest to note the attempt described in the contributions from China and Taiwan to develop an IP for all of the Chinese societies. Still, even in the Chinese context different approaches to the IP among the contributors were noticeable. In addition, this discussion illustrates that the dimensions along which new IPs develop may vary, for example, with respect to the role of religion, or the approach to the philosophy of science that is promoted, or the methodological preferences (see also Allwood, 2002). In this context it is also of interest that one contribution, given today's globalized world, even doubted the value of basing IPs "on fixed ethnic entities."

As all of these themes show, the overview and discussion in this article has revealed that the IPs are an exciting and creative addition to contemporary psychology.

REFERENCES

Abbott, M., & Durie, M. H. (1987). A whiter shade of pale: Taha Maori and professional psychology training. *New Zealand Journal of Psychology, 16,* 58–71.

Allwood, C. M. (1998). The creation and nature(s) of indigenized psychologies from the perspective of the anthropology of knowledge. In S. Gorenstein (Ed.), *Knowledge and society, Vol. 11* (pp. 153–172). Greenwich, CT: Jai Press.

Allwood, C. M. (2002). Indigenized psychologies. *Social Epistemology, 16,* 349–366.

Allwood, C. M., & Hakken, D. (2001). "Use" discourses in system development: Can communication be improved? *AI & Technology, 15,* 169–199.

Atal, Y. (1974). The call for indigenization. In V. Enriquez (Ed.), *Indigenous psychology: A book of readings* (pp. 31–50). Akademya ng Sikolohiyang Pilipino. Quezon City, The Philippines: Philippine Psychology Research & Training House.

Bandura, A. (1997). *Self-efficacy: The exercise of control.* New York: Freeman.

Berry, J. W. (1974). Canadian psychology: Some social and applied emphases. *Canadian Psychologist, 15,* 132–139.

Berry, J. W. (1983). The sociogenesis of social sciences: An analysis of the cultural relativity of social psychology. In B. Bain (Ed.), *The sociogenesis of language and human conduct* (pp. 449–458). New York: Plenum Press.

Berry, J. W., & Kim, U. (1993). The way ahead: From indigenous psychologies to a universal psychology. In U. Kim & J. W. Berry (Eds.), *Indigenous psychologies: Research and experience in cultural context* (pp. 277–280). Newbury Park, CA: Sage.

Berry, J. W., Poortinga, Y. H., Segall, M. H., & Dasen, P. R. (2002) *Cross-cultural psychology: Research and applications* (2nd ed.). New York: Cambridge University Press.

Berry, J. W., & Wilde, G. J. S. (Eds.). (1972). *Social psychology: The Canadian context.* Toronto: McClelland & Stewart.

Bhawuk, D. P. S. (1999). Who attains peace: An Indian model of personal harmony. *Indian Psychological Review, 52,* 40–48.

Borofsky, R. (1987). *Making history: Pukapukan and anthropological constructions of knowledge.* New York: Cambridge University Press.

Boski, P. (1993). Between West and East: Humanist values and concerns in Polish psychology. In U. Kim & J. W. Berry (Eds.), *Indigenous psychologies* (pp. 79–103). Newbury Park, CA: Sage.

Boski, P. (2002). Cultural alternative to comparative social psychology. In P. Boski, F. J. R. van de Vijver, & A. M. Chodynicka (Eds.), *New directions in cross-cultural psychology* (pp. 55–69). Warszawa: Wydawnictwo Instytutu Psychologii PAN.

Boski, P. (in press). Humanism-materialism: Polish cultural origins and cross-cultural comparisons. In U. Kim & K. S. Yang (Eds.), *Scientific advances in indigenous psychologies.* Cambridge: Cambridge University Press.

Boski, P., Van de Vijver, F. J. R., Hurme, H., & Miluska, J. (1999). Perception and evaluation of Polish cultural femininity in Poland, the USA, Finland, and the Netherlands. *Cross-Cultural Research, 33,* 131–161.

Cheung, F. M., Cheung, S. F., Wada, S., & Zhang, J. X. (2003). Indigenous measures of personality assessment in Asian countries: A review. *Psychological Assessment, 15,* 280–289.

Cheung, F. M., Leung, K., Zhang, J. X., Sun, H. F., Gan, Y. Q., Song, W. Z., & Xie, D. (2001). Indigenous Chinese personality constructs: Is the Five Factor Model complete? *Journal of Cross-Cultural Psychology, 32,* 407–433.

Choi, S. C., Kim, U., & Kim, D. I. (1997). Multifaceted analyses of chemyon ("social face"): An indigenous Korean perspective. In K. Leung, U. Kim, S. Yamaguchi, & Y. Kashima (Eds.), *Progress in Asian social psychologies.* Singapore: John Wiley.

Church, A. T., & Katigbak, M. S. (2002). Indigenization of psychology in the Philippines. *International Journal of Psychology, 37,* 129–148.

Cole, M. (1996). *Cultural psychology: A once and future discipline.* Cambridge, MA: The Belknap Press of Harvard University Press.

Durie, M. H. (1994). *Whaiora: Maori health development.* Auckland, New Zealand: Oxford University Press.

Durojaiye, M. O. (1993). Indigenous psychology in Africa: The search for meaning. In U. Kim & J. W. Berry (Eds.), *Indigenous psychologies: Research and experience in cultural context* (pp. 211–220). Newbury Park, CA: Sage.

Enriquez, V. G. (1985). *Kapwa*: A core concept in Filipino social psychology In A. Aganon & S. M. Assumpta David (Eds.). *Sikolohiyang Pilipino: Isyu, Pananaw, at Kaalaman* (New directions in indigenous psychology). Quezon City, The Philippines: National Book Store.

Enriquez, V. G. (1992). *From colonial to liberation psychology: The Philippine experience*. Quezon City, The Philippines: University of the Philippines Press.

Enriquez, V. G. (1993). Developing a Filipino psychology. In U. Kim & J. W. Berry (Eds.), *Indigenous psychologies: Research and experience in cultural context* (pp. 152–169). Newbury Park, CA: Sage.

Feliciano, G. D. (1965). The limits of Western social research methods in rural Philippines: The need for innovation. In R. G. Pe-Pua (Ed.), *Filipino psychology: Theory, method and application* (pp. 99–110). Quezon City, The Philippines: University of the Philippines Press.

Ghamari-Tabrizi, B. (1996). Is Islamic science possible? *Social Epistemology* [Special issue*: Islamic social epistemology*], *10*, 317–330.

Giere, R. N. (Ed.). (1992). *Cognitive models of science. Minnesota Studies in the Philosophy of Science*. Minneapolis, MN: University of Minnesota Press.

Hamerton, H., Nikora, L. W., Robertson, N., & Thomas, D. R. (1994). Community psychology in Aotearoa/New Zealand. *The Community Psychologist, 28*, 21–23.

Heelas, P., & Lock, A. (Eds.). (1981). *Indigenous psychologies: The anthropology of self*. London: Academic Press.

Ho, D. Y. F. (1988). Asian psychology. A dialogue in indigenization and beyond. In A. C. Paranjpe, D. Y. F. Ho, & R. W. Rieber (Eds.), *Asian contributions to psychology* (pp. 53–77). New York: Praeger.

Hwang, K. K. (1987). Face and favor: The Chinese power game. *American Journal of Sociology, 92*, 945–974.

Hwang, K. K. (1995). *Knowledge and action: A social-psychological interpretation of Chinese cultural tradition* [In Chinese]. Taipei: Sin-Li.

Hwang, K. K. (1997–8). *Guanxiand* and *mientze*: Conflict resolution in Chinese society. *Intercultural Communication Studies, 7*, 17–37.

Hwang, K. K. (1998). Two moralities: Reinterpreting the finding of empirical research on moral reasoning in Taiwan. *Asian Journal of Social Psychology, 1*, 211–238.

Hwang, K. K. (2000). Chinese relationalism: Theoretical construction and methodological considerations. *Journal for the Theory of Social Behavior, 30*, 155–178.

Hwang, K. K. (2001). The deep structure of Confucianism: A social psychological approach. *Asian Philosophy, 11*, 179–204.

Hwang, K. K. (2005). From anticolonialism to postcolonialism: Emergence of Chinese indigenous psychology in Taiwan. *International Journal of Psychology, 40*, 228–238.

Hwang, K. K. (in press-a). A philosophical reflection on the epistemology and methodology of indigenous psychology. *Asian Journal of Social Psychology*.

Hwang, K. K. (in press-b). Epistemological goal of indigenous psychology: A perspective from constructive realism. In B. N. Setiadi, A. Supratiknya, W. J. S. Lonner, & Y. H. Poortinga (Eds.), *Unity in diversity: Enhancing a peaceful world*. Proceedings of the XVIth International Congress of IACCP.

Hwang, K. K., & Yang, C.-F. (Eds.). (2000). *Asian Journal of Social Psychology* [Special issue: Indigenous, cultural and cross-cultural psychologies], *3*.

Kakar, S. (1978). *The inner world: A psychoanalytic study of childhood and society in India*. Delhi: Oxford University Press.

Kao, H. S. R. (1989). Insights towards a transcultural psychology: Spotlighting the Middle Kingdom. Supplement to *The Gazette* (University of Hong Kong), *36*, 85–92.

Kao, H. S. R., & Sinha, D. (1997). *Asian perspectives on psychology* (pp. 9–12, 26–32, 34–39). New Delhi/Thousand Oaks, CA/London: Sage.

Kim, U. (2001). Culture, science and indigenous psychologies: An integrated analysis. In D. Matsumoto (Ed.), *Handbook of culture and psychology* (pp. 51–76). Oxford: Oxford University Press.

Kim, U., & Berry, J. W. (1993). *Indigenous psychologies: Experience and research in cultural context*. Newbury Park, CA: Sage.

Kim, U., & Yang, K. (Eds.). (in press). *Scientific advances in indigenous psychologies*. Cambridge: Cambridge University Press.

Kitayama, S., & Markus, H. R. (2000). The pursuit of happiness and the realization of sympathy: Cutural patterns of self, social relations, and well-being. In E. Diener & E. M. Suh (Eds.), *Culture and subjective well-being* (pp. 113–162). Cambridge, MA: MIT Press.

Levy, M. (2002). *Barriers and incentives to Maori participation in the profession of psychology: A report prepared for the New Zealand Psychologists Board*. Wellington, New Zealand: NZ Psychologists Board.

Lundberg, I. (2001). Zeitgeist, Ortgeist, and personalities in the development of Scandinavian psychology. *International Journal of Psychology, 36*, 356–362.

Marai, L. (1997). The development of psychology in Papua New Guinea: A brief review. *South Pacific Journal of Psychology, 7*, 1–6.

Matsumoto, D. (Ed.). (2001). *The handbook of culture and psychology*. New York: Oxford University Press.

Middleton, D., & Edwards, D. (Eds.). (1990). *Collective remembering*. London: Sage.

Mignolo, W. D. (1998). Globalization, civilization processes, and the relocation of languages and cultures. In F. Jameson & M. Miyoshi (Eds.), *The cultures of globalization* (pp. 31–53). Durham, NC: Duke University Press.

Ministry of Education, (1995). *National Forum on Education, 1995*. Yaounde, Cameroon: Author.

Moghaddam, F. M. (1987). Psychology in the Three Worlds: As reflected by the crisis in social psychology and the move toward indigenous Third-World psychology. *American Psychologist, 42*, 912–920.

Moghaddam, F. M. (2002). *The individual and society: A cultural integration*. New York: Worth.

Moghaddam, F. M., & Taylor, D. M. (1986). What constitutes an 'appropriate psychology' for the developing world? *International Journal of Psychology, 21*, 253–267.

Moscovici, S. (1972). Society and theory in social psychology. In J. Israel & H. Tajfel (Eds.), *The context of social psychology* (pp. 17–68). London: Academic Press.

Mulkay, M. J. (1972). *The social process of innovation.* London: Macmillan.

Mundy-Castle, A. C. (1974). Social and technological intelligence in Western and non-Western cultures. *Universitas, 4,* 46–52.

Nikora, L. W. (2001). Rangatiratanga-Kawanatanga: Dealing with rhetoric. *Feminism & Psychology, 11,* 377–385.

Nikora, L. W., Levy, M., Masters, B., Waitoki, M., Te Awekotuku, N., & Etheredge, R. J. M. (Eds.). (2003). *The Proceedings of the National Maori Graduates of Psychology Symposium 2002: Making a difference.* Waikato, New Zealand: Maori & Psychology Research Unit, University of Waikato.

Nisbett, R. E. (2003). *The geography of thought.* New York: Free Press.

Nsamenang, A. B. (1992). *Human development in cultural context: A Third World perspective.* Newbury Park, CA: Sage.

Nsamenang, A. B. (1993). Psychology in sub-Saharan Africa. *Psychology in Developing Societies, 5,* 171–184.

Nsamenang, A. B. (1995). Factors influencing the development of psychology in Sub-Saharan Africa. *International Journal of Psychology, 30,* 729–739.

Nsamenang, A. B. (2001). Indigenous view on human development: A West African perspective. In N. J. Smelser & P. B. Baltes (Eds.-in-Chief) (Eds.), *International encyclopedia of the social and behavioral sciences.* London: Elsevier.

Nsamenang, A. B., & Dasen, P. R. (Guest Eds.). (1993). Special Issue*: Journal of Psychology in Africa: Child Development & National Development in Cameroon, 1*(5).

Ord, G. (1972). Testing for educational and occupational selection in developing countries. *Occupational Psychology, 46*(3).

Pande, N., & Naidu, R. K. (1992). *Anasakti* and health: A study of non-attachment. *Psychology and Developing Societies, 4,* 89–104.

Pandey, J. (Ed.). (1988). *Psychology in India: The state-of-the-art* (3 volumes). New Delhi: Sage.

Ritchie, J. E. (1992). *Becoming bicultural.* Wellington, New Zealand: Huia Publishers with Daphne Brasell Associates.

Salazar, Z. (1991). *Ang pantayong pananaw bilang diskursong pangkabihasnan* [The *pantayo* perspective as cultural discourse]. In V. Bautista & R. Pe-Pua (Eds.), *Philippine studies: History, philosophy and research.* Manila: Kalikasan Press.

Serpell, R., & Akkari, A. (2001). Qualitative approaches to cultural psychology: A point of entry for egalitarian cross-cultural communication among researchers. In M. Lahlou & G. Vinsonneau (Eds.), *La Psychologie au regard des contacts de cultures.* Limonest, France: L'Interdisciplinaire.

Shadish, W., & Fuller, S. (Eds.). (1994). *The social psychology of science.* New York: Guilford Press.

Sinha, D. (1996). Cross-cultural psychology: The Asian scenario. In J. Pandey, D. Sinha, & D. P. S. Bhawuk (Eds.), *Asian contributions to cross-cultural psychology* (pp. 20–41). New Delhi/Thousand Oaks, CA/London: Sage.

Sinha, D. (1997). Indigenizing psychology. In J. W. Berry, Y. H. Poortinga, & J. Pandey (Eds.), *Handbook of cross-cultural psychology* (pp. 130–169). Boston: Allyn & Bacon.

Sinha, J. B. P. (1995). *The cultural context of leadership and power.* New Delhi: Sage.

Sinha, J. B. P. (2003). Trends towards indigenization of psychology in India. In K. S. Yang, K. K. Hwang, P. Pederson, & I. Diabo (Eds.), *Progress in Asian psychology: Conceptual and empirical contributions* (pp. 11–28). Westport, CT & London: Praeger.

Taylor, C. A. (1996). *Defining science: A rhetoric of demarcation.* Madison, WI: The University of Wisconsin Press.

Wierzbicka, A. (1999). *Emotions across languages and cultures.* Cambridge: Cambridge University Press.

Yang, K. S. (1993). Why do we need to develop an indigenous Chinese psychology? *Indigenous Psychological Research in Chinese Societies* [in Chinese], *1,* 6–88.

Yang, K. S. (1997). Indigenizing Westernized Chinese psychology. In M. H. Bond (Ed.), *Working at the interface of cultures: Eighteen lives in social science* (pp. 62–76). New York: Routledge.

Yang, K. S. (1999). Towards an indigenous Chinese psychology: A selective review of methodological, theoretical, and empirical accomplishments. *Chinese Journal of Psychology, 41,* 181–211.

Yang, K. S. (2000). Monocultural and cross-cultural indigenous approaches: The royal road to the development of a balanced global psychology. *Asian Journal of Social Psychology, 3,* 241–263.

Ziman, J. M. (1995). *Of one mind: The collectivization of science.* Woodbury, NY: American Institute of Physics Press.

Ziman, J. M. (2000). *Real science.* Cambridge: Cambridge University Press.

INTERNATIONAL JOURNAL OF PSYCHOLOGY, 2006, 41 (4), 269–275

Comment

Kurt Danziger

York University, Toronto, Canada, and University of Cape Town, South Africa

*F*or some contributors, "indigenous psychology" seems to involve no more than the introduction of essentially technical modifications that serve to enhance the export value of psychological products imported from the West. For the majority, however, indigenous psychology seems to imply some kind of reaction against the way in which the ideal of universal psychological knowledge is commonly pursued in the major centres. Insofar as this reaction is concerned with fundamental issues, it can be seen as questioning the social and normative framework within which psychological knowledge is produced and evaluated. Certain culture-bound interpretations of science and scientific method form an important part of this framework. Although complaints about the individualistic bias of Western psychology are common, there is a need for further exploration of the link between this brand of individualism, "Cartesian psychology," and a certain understanding of the goals of scientific investigation in psychology. These goals, as well as the norms governing their practical pursuit, are embedded in and enforced by disciplinary structures that are now international in scope but were originally the product of quite specific historical circumstances. This imported disciplinary organization of psychological knowledge may not be appropriate at all times and everywhere. It may be particularly inappropriate where the primary task of indigenous psychology is considered to be the generation of locally appropriate knowledge. Another obstacle to the achievement of this task is constituted by the uncritical use of "culture" as an entity. A more promising approach is provided by those contributors for whom indigenous psychology means doing research *with* rather than *on* indigenous people. This seems to be an important step towards escaping a tradition in which the human sources and the human beneficiaries of professional psychological knowledge have seldom been the same people.

*P*our certains collaborateurs, la «psychologie indigène» semble impliquer pas plus que l'introduction de modifications techniques essentielles servant à améliorer la valeur d'exportation des produits psychologiques importés de l'Ouest. Pour la majorité, cependant, la psychologie indigène semble impliquer une sorte de réaction envers la façon dont la connaissance psychologique idéale et universelle est communément poursuivie dans les principaux centres. Considérant le fait que cette réaction concerne des enjeux fondamentaux, elle peut être perçue comme une remise en question du cadre de travail social et normatif dans lequel la connaissance psychologique est produite et évaluée. Certaines interprétations présentent des limites culturelles relativement à la science et à la méthode scientifique constituent une partie importante de ce cadre de travail. Quoique des récriminations vis-à-vis les biais individualistes de la psychologie occidentale soient communes, il y a un besoin d'explorer plus loin le lien entre cette marque d'individualisme, la «psychologie cartésienne» et une certaine compréhension des buts de la recherche en psychologie. Ces buts, tout comme les normes gouvernant leur poursuite pratique, sont enchâssés dans, et forcés par, des structures disciplinaires qui sont maintenant d'envergure internationale, mais qui étaient originairement le produit de circonstances historiques plus spécifiques. Cette organisation disciplinaire importée de la connaissance psychologique peut ne pas être appropriée n'importe où et n'importe quand. Cela peut être particulièrement inapproprié où le devoir principal de la psychologie indigène est considéré comme étant la production d'une connaissance localement appropriée. Un autre obstacle à l'atteinte de ce devoir consiste en l'utilisation non critique de la «culture» en tant qu'entité. Une approche plus prometteuse est fournie par les collaborateurs pour lesquels la psychologie indigène signifie faire de la recherche *avec* plutôt que *sur* le peuple indigène. Ceci semble être une étape importante pour échapper à une tradition dans laquelle les sources humaines et les bénéficiaires humains de la connaissance psychologique professionnelle ont rarement été le même peuple.

Correspondence should be addressed to Kurt Danziger, 32 Greengate Road, Toronto, Canada. (E-mail: kdanzig@yorku.ca).

http://www.psypress.com/ijp   DOI: 10.1080/00207590544000031

*P*ara algunos de los autores de este número, la «psicología tradicional» parece implicar algo más que la introducción de modificaciones técnicas esenciales que sirvan para mejorar el valor de exportación de los productos psicológicos importados de Occidente. Para la mayoría, sin embargo, la psicología tradicional parece implicar una especie de reacción hacia el modo en que suele buscarse el conocimiento psicológico ideal y universal en los principales centros. Considerando el hecho de que esta reacción implica problemas fundamentales, puede ser vista como un cuestionamiento del esquema de trabajo social y normativo en el cual se produce y se evalúa el conocimiento psicológico. Algunas interpretaciones de la ciencia y el método científico limitadas por la cultura son parte importante de este esquema de trabajo. A pesar de que las quejas contra las tendencias individualistas de la psicología son comunes, es necesario sin embargo explorar aún más a fondo el vínculo entre esta marca de individualismo, la «psicología cartesiana» y una cierta comprensión de las metas de la investigación en psicología. Estas metas, al igual que las normas que regulan su trabajo de búsqueda en la práctica, están encasilladas y se ven reforzadas por estructuras disciplinarias que son, hoy en día, de alcance internacional, pero que eran originalmente producto de circunstancias históricas más específicas. Esta organización disciplinaria importada del conocimiento psicológico puede no ser apropiada en todo momento y en cualquier lugar. Esto puede ser particularmente inapropiado cuando se considera que el deber principal de la psicología tradicional es la generación de un conocimiento apropiado a nivel local. Otro obstáculo para el cumplimiento de este deber consiste en la utilización no crítica de la «cultura» como entidad. Una aproximación más prometedora proviene de aquellos colaboradores para quienes la psicología tradicional significa realizar la investigación *con* la población tradicional, y no tanto *acerca* de la población tradicional. Esto parece ser un paso importante para escapar a una tradición en la cual los recursos humanos y los beneficiarios humanos del conocimiento psicológico profesional son rara vez las mismas personas.

I was first brought up against the reality of indigenous psychology nearly half a century ago when I was working at an Indonesian University. I found to my great surprise that I had an Indonesian colleague who was already teaching courses on a kind of psychology based on a vernacular literature, the roots of which went back many centuries (Danziger, 1997). Since then, the challenge of indigenous psychologies (though they were not always called that) has been a significant presence for me while teaching and doing psychological research in five continents. Being confronted by the existence of psychologies that were often vastly different from the Anglo-American psychology in which I had been trained decisively influenced the direction of my own work and turned me towards a study of the historical emergence of "Western" psychological theory and practice. My comments on the present discussion are informed by this background; they are not those of an active participant in the field but of an outsider with some personal experience of the issues and a perspective that is historical and philosophical rather than culturological.

VERSIONS OF INDIGENOUS PSYCHOLOGY

Plurality and heterogeneity seem to be necessary and essential features of the field of indigenous psychology. Nevertheless, all indigenous psychologies seem to share a common metaphor, that of the local versus the distant. The nature of the

"local" is exceedingly diverse, covering many very different parts of the world, and ranging from ethnic minorities to large national entities. Indigenous psychologies profess a certain sensitivity to the local and therefore manifest great diversity. They also differ significantly in the way the relationship between the local and the distant is conceived.

In some cases the relationship is presented as though there were no fundamental incompatibility between work originating in different localities. In the extreme version of this interpretation, psychologies are regarded as "indigenous" merely in the sense that they all have some local origin, whether that origin is defined in terms of the borders of a country, some cultural entity, or a particular academic institution. Indigenous psychology then becomes little more than another, more fashionable, term for what E. G. Boring (1950) used to call *Ortsgeist*, the counterpart to his more famous *Zeitgeist*.

Although there are echoes of this use of "indigenous" in some of the contributions to this discussion, especially those from the so-called "West," the majority present a different picture. Here, indigenous psychology is characterized by some form of opposition to, rejection of, or simply distancing from a way of doing psychology that is characterized as Western or American. Indigenous psychology in this sense is a *reaction* to a particular stimulus, where "stimulus" is to be taken in its ancient meaning of "irritant." This reaction calls for changes that take two forms, *technical* and *structural*. Technical changes become necessary because modern psychology is an article of export from one part of the world to another. Even material exports often require modification to make them useful under new local conditions. That cultural exports should experience the same fate is hardly a cause for surprise.

Indeed, the "indigenous" component in some versions of indigenous psychology appears to be quite analogous to the technical changes that are often necessary before Western-designed machinery can work effectively in less industrialized parts of the world. This is essentially what happens when standard psychological assessment techniques are modified for use in countries of "the East" or "the South" by adding or deleting certain items and scales, or introducing new quantified "dimensions" of personality or social interaction. It is also what happens when these modified techniques are applied to solve research questions that have not simply been imported unchanged from abroad but have been modified in the light of local issues and priorities. In that case the term "indigenous psychology" is merely used to refer to a psychology whose export value has been enhanced by locally appropriate modifications but that is indistinguishable on any fundamental criterion from its Western prototype.

However, for many contributors the issues that arise in the process of indigenization cannot be reduced to technical problems but involve decisions grounded in questions of cultural identity and historically evolved power relationships. In the case of material goods, the export of specific items of technology always takes place within a socioeconomic framework that constitutes the world trade system. That system operates according to rules that are the product of historically inherited structures of inequality. Remarks by some of the contributors suggest that the export of cultural goods, such as the techniques and concepts of "Western" or "American" psychology, also takes place within a framework of historically derived asymmetric relationships. For instance, Western texts and journals are far more widely disseminated and are consulted far more frequently and seriously than their non-Western counterparts, and students commonly travel to the West, not the East or South, for their professional socialization as psychologists.

Much of this asymmetry can be accounted for in economic terms: World resources for the production of psychological knowledge and the training of professional psychologists are very unequally distributed. The flow of information is skewed in that much more is exported from the most developed centres than is imported by them. But these centres not only produce a lot of potentially exportable psychological knowledge, they also invented and exported the *criteria* by which the value of the products of psychological research are judged within the profession. These criteria are as closely tied to the cultural context of their origin, as is the specific content of exported psychological knowledge. Yet, after they have been exported, these criteria provide the standard for judging the value of psychological knowledge produced anywhere. The result is that the products of the major exporting centres commonly achieve an exemplary or paradigmatic value that other producers will hope to approximate unless they reject the criteria on which the system of evaluation is based. This rejection is central to the project of indigenous psychology in its more radical forms.

In the present set of contributions, the more radical aspirations of indigenous psychology are addressed primarily in three contexts, which may be conveniently identified by means of the keywords *science*, *disciplinarity*, and *voice*. I will address these in turn.

Science

Apart from some marginalized exceptions modern (Western) psychology understands itself as an essentially *scientific* project and is so perceived by others. Its cognitive authority and the plausibility of its knowledge claims derive from this essential scientificity. No doubt, the historical link to science has been advantageous to the development of psychology as an academic discipline in the West. But in opting for this path psychologists have also had to accept certain restrictions. One major restriction pertains to the kind of knowledge that their discipline is designed to foster. Scientific knowledge is regarded as the only legitimate kind of knowledge in a disciplinary context, though in other life contexts individual psychologists may well appreciate the value of other kinds of knowledge.

On the orthodox view, "science" functions as a source of regulative norms for the conduct of psychological inquiry. These norms prescribe the kind of knowledge that is sought after and the means for attaining it. When modern psychology was transplanted from its countries of origin to other regions of the world, not only specific items of knowledge and specific instruments travelled; certain norms for the conduct of psychological inquiry, and certain criteria for assessing the legitimacy of forms of psychological knowledge, travelled too. The application of these norms and criteria imparted a particular character to the export as a whole. Only insofar as indigenous psychology proceeds to a questioning of these norms and criteria does it represent a real challenge to the status quo in the asymmetric global circulation of psychological knowledge and practice.

There are indications that some representatives of indigenous psychology are not unaware of the problematic aspects of Western psychology's scientific pretensions. K.-K. Hwang, for instance, distinguishes scientific knowledge as a specific type of knowledge and recognizes that indigenous psychology has epistemological goals. U. Kim refers to "the Euro-American values that champion individualistic, de-contextualized, and analytical knowledge."

However, for many representatives of indigenous psychology, as indeed for most of their Western colleagues, "science" continues to be an uncontroversial, unexamined, source of cognitive authority. As Allwood (2002) has pointed out, this is likely to create problems for the field. Insofar as indigenous psychologists emphasize the cultural embeddedness of psychology while proceeding as though "science" was entirely separate from culture, they are likely to become deeply embroiled in paradox (see Harding, 1998). One has to distinguish between *science* in some ideal Platonic sense and the numerous historical versions of "science" that have often differed from each other to the point of incompatibility (Fuller, 2002). One of these versions acquired canonical status in American psychology around the middle of the 20th century and was then exported together with the psychology for which it supplied the regulative norms of legitimate practice. It cannot be emphasized too strongly that this version of scientific practice, whose peculiarities have been widely noted (see, e.g., Michell, 2000; Tolman, 1991), was no less a product of specific social circumstances and cultural traditions than the psychological content to which it was applied.

As the editors of this collection noted in their introductory comments, the broader issues entailed here have provided grist for an extensive field of science studies (see Golinski, 1998; Harding, 1998; and Pickering, 1992, for particularly relevant material). Deeper links with this field would help to face the challenges of what one of the contributors refers to as a "truly universal" psychological understanding. To ground such an understanding in a universalized understanding of science is to build on shifting sands, for codes of scientific practice are not and never have been unified except as myth (Galison & Stump, 1996).

The notion of a universal psychology appears to hold an abiding attraction for most contributors. Possibly this attraction derives from a faith in the psychic unity of humankind, which is certainly preferable to the sorts of prejudice that flourished in the period of colonialism. What is questionable is any implication that a particular historically constituted version of the norms of scientific practice represents the royal road to the discovery of humankind's psychic unity.

Adherence to the ideal of "a universal psychology" seems almost as common as a rejection of the "individualism" of Western psychology. Yet, in the history of Western psychology, individualism and the search for universal laws have been closely linked: Psychological laws would be considered universal insofar as they applied to all individuals or to quantifiable differences among individuals along a common set of dimensions. Is it possible to break this link between individualism and universalism, as the remarks of several contributors seem to require?

I think this is certainly possible, once it is recognized that both individualism and universalism come in a number of versions. In traditional Western psychology, a particular version of universalism is linked to a particular form of individualism in a combination that is deeply engrained in the discipline's investigative practices. This combination takes the form of what has been called "Cartesian psychology" (Wilson, 1995), based on the belief that the scientific generalizations of psychology pertain to intra-individual processes and characteristics. Examples of these are variables of personality and intelligence as well as most of what has been investigated under "cognitive processes." The Western cultural roots of Cartesian psychology are glaringly obvious, yet its preconceptions are so deeply enmeshed with the procedural norms of traditional scientific psychology that alternative approaches have long been subject to disciplinary marginalization.

As several contributors note, the psychology that had its origins in and flourished in Western societies reflects the values of those societies to a degree that it too can be considered an indigenous psychology. Perhaps one could say that traditional or "mainstream" psychology has respected only one form of indigenous psychology, which it then attempted to universalize. Abandoning this path towards creating a universal psychology does not mean abandoning the possibility of any kind of general validity for psychological concepts. But it does mean abandoning terms that refer solely to the insides of isolated heads or the qualities of autonomous individuals. Variations in the social and environmental conditions under which individuals act are not separate items to be added *after* "basic" psychological uniformities have been established, they are an intrinsic aspect of human activity. Taking such considerations seriously results in a redefinition of psychology's subject matter and a change in the paradigm of psychological research. Topics such as "distributed cognition" (Hutchins, 1995), "situated cognition" (Clancy, 1997), "situated learning" (Lave & Wenger, 1991), "distributed intelligence" (Pea, 1993), provide salient examples (see also Schliemann & Carraher, 2001). A dialogue between these approaches and various indigenous psychologies may be an important step towards a psychology that is not based on an individualistic metaphysic.

Discipline

Discussions of indigenous psychology, including the present one, usually take place in a *disciplinary* context: The contributors have received their professional socialization as psychologists; the medium of publication is a psychological journal or book; and so the primary audience is also one of professional psychologists and candidate psychologists. Consequently, much of the discussion typically revolves around the relation of indigenous psychology to the *discipline* of psychology, whether in terms of its past, present, or future.

It is only in historically rather recent times that the academic or scientific discipline has become the dominant institutional form that provides the framework within which the generation of scientific knowledge takes place. For about a century in America, and less in Europe, disciplinary structures have presided over professional socialization, controlled prestigious publications, affected the career chances of individual members of the discipline, influenced the flow of research funds, and so on. These activities depend on the development of a *normative* framework that is characteristic of each discipline. Different disciplines still embody different conceptions of what it means to do good research, what procedures are regarded as being scientific or objective, what the knowledge products of the discipline should look like, and where the discipline's boundaries are drawn, as well as other normative canons. Typically, this gives rise to a "regression into professional purity" (Abbott, 2000), a tendency to do

work that embodies this normative framework visibly and rigidly.

The disciplinary organization of knowledge was exported to much of the world in the course of imperial rule. In the case of psychology, the major push towards the internationalization of disciplinary authority did not take place until the second half of the 20th century, by which time American psychology had come to be the dominant factor in the discipline on a global scale. As many of the contributions to the present discussion indicate, indigenous psychology represents some kind of reaction to this development.

There is, however, a tendency to formulate the reaction in purely cognitive terms and to pay less attention to the institutional aspects of the disciplinization of knowledge. It cannot be taken for granted that the disciplinary division of scientific authority, which evolved under specific historical circumstances, has a timeless value for all times and places (Staeuble, 2004). On the contrary, the experience of several contributors suggests rather that disciplinary norms and disciplinary authority have often become a means for extending the global reach of certain ideals for organizing social and economic life. It is surprising, therefore, that so few contributors address the question of changing psychology's disciplinary boundaries and primary disciplinary affiliations in the course of indigenization, J. B. P. Sinha being a notable exception. It seems that alternatives to imported patterns of disciplinary organization at least deserve serious examination if indigenous psychology is to flourish.

Voice

The term "indigenous psychology" is not always used in a disciplinary context, but can also be used to refer to psychological usage or understanding among scientifically untrained lay people in their daily lives. This ambiguity points to the existence of two sources from which work in this area derives its legitimation. When "indigenous psychology" is used primarily in the sense of a body of explicitly formulated objective knowledge, it is a matter of establishing its scientific credentials before the court of disciplinary authority. When the same term is used primarily to refer to the everyday psychology of people of a certain background, the crucial issue is one of asserting the value of *their* understanding of human life and rescuing it from oblivion; of giving voice to those who are not professionally certified. This emerges most clearly in the contributions from Africa (Nsamenang) and New Zealand, for which indigenous psychology becomes a way of generating locally relevant knowledge and practice by privileging the input of local people; doing research *with* rather than *on* indigenous people, as the Maori research group put it.

This touches on quite a profound, though largely unacknowledged, division between two understandings of indigenous psychology. For many, the field is defined in terms of the concept of "culture" and its problems arise out of the existence of "cultural differences." I would not be the first to remark upon the irony of this emerging emphasis on culture in a world in which traditional cultural differences are being eroded at an unprecedented rate and in which cultural hybridization and interpenetration is so common (Hermans & Kempen, 1998). For this reason it is not obvious that the reification of culture, in terms of geographically based and essentialist entities, offers the most promising basis for the development of indigenous psychologies. The discipline of anthropology, which virtually invented "culture" in its modern sense, has certainly become much more cautious about the "territorialized" and reified use of that concept (e.g. Kuper, 1999), still very common among psychologists.

Ultimately, it is people, and not cultures understood as entities, which constitute the units of analysis. Of course, it is taken for granted that people are cultural beings, but not in the sense that they are the "dopes" of homogeneous cultural traditions. Their "indigenous" psychologies usually represent an often inharmonious and unstable mixture of cultural elements. As an area of investigative practice, indigenous psychology would have the task of doing justice to this complex mixture and thus to give voice to people too often silenced by a homogenizing world system.

In the end, indigenous psychology seems to be faced by the question: Psychology for whom? The vague hope that psychological knowledge will be good for humankind should not prevent recognition of the fact that, in principle, this knowledge can be used in two ways. It can be used to exert control over others (for their own good, it is claimed), or it can be used as a resource for self-growth. That distinction applies to communities as well as to individuals. In the past, a great deal of psychological research has been geared to producing the kind of knowledge that would be useful primarily to experts working in institutional contexts dedicated to the administration of human resources and human inadequacies (Danziger,

1990). The knowledge that was initially exported to colonies and quasi-colonies was almost all of this kind (Smith, 1999). Indigenization, however, carries the promise of knowledge that is more adequate to goals of individual and community emancipation.

REFERENCES

Abbott, A. (2000). *Chaos of disciplines*. Chicago: Chicago University Press.

Allwood, C. M. (2002). Indigenized psychologies. *Social Epistemology, 16*, 349–366.

Boring, E. G. (1950). *A history of experimental psychology* (2nd ed.). New York: Appleton-Century-Crofts.

Clancy, W. J. (1997). *Situated cognition: On human knowledge and computer representation*. Cambridge: Cambridge University Press.

Danziger, K. (1990). *Constructing the subject: Historical origins of psychological research*. Cambridge: Cambridge University Press.

Danziger, K. (1997). *Naming the mind: How psychology found its language*. London: Sage.

Fuller, S. (2002). *Social epistemology* (2nd ed.). Bloomington, IN: Indiana University Press.

Galison, P., & Stump, D. J. (1996). *The disunity of science: Boundaries, contexts, and power*. Stanford, CA: Stanford University Press.

Golinski, J. (1998). *Making natural knowledge: Constructivism and the history of science*. Cambridge: Cambridge University Press.

Harding, S. (1998). *Is science multi-cultural? Postcolonialisms, feminisms, and epistemologies*. Bloomington, IN: Indiana University Press.

Hermans, J. M., & Kempen, H. J. G. (1998). Moving cultures: The perilous problems of cultural dichotomies in a globalizing society. *American Psychologist, 53*, 1111–1120.

Hutchins, E. (1995). *Cognition in the wild*. Cambridge, MA: MIT Press.

Kuper, A. (1999). *Culture: The anthropologists' account*. Cambridge, MA: Harvard University Press.

Lave, J., & Wenger, E. (1991). *Situated learning: Legitimate peripheral participation*. Cambridge: Cambridge University Press.

Michell, J. (2000). Normal science, pathological science and psychometrics. *Theory and Psychology, 10*, 639–667.

Pea, R. D. (1993). Practices of distributed intelligence and designs for education. In G. Salomon (Ed.), *Distributed cognitions: Psychological and educational considerations* (pp. 47–87). Cambridge: Cambridge University Press.

Pickering, A. (1992). *Science as practice and culture*. Chicago: Chicago University Press.

Schliemann, A. D., & Carraher, D. W. (2001). Everyday cognition: Where culture, psychology and education come together. In D. Matsumoto (Ed.), *The handbook of culture and psychology* (pp. 137–150). New York: Oxford University Press.

Smith, L. T. (1999). Decolonizing methodologies: Research and indigenous peoples. London: Zed Books.

Staeuble, I. (2004). De-centering Western perspectives: Psychology and the disciplinary order in the first and third world. In A. C. Brock, J. Louw, & W. van Hoorn (Eds.), *Rediscovering the history of psychology: Essays inspired by the work of Kurt Danziger* (pp. 183–205). New York: Kluwer.

Tolman, C. (1991). *Positivism in psychology*. New York: Springer.

Wilson, R. A. (1995). *Cartesian psychology and physical minds: Individualism and the sciences of the mind*. Cambridge: Cambridge University Press.

INTERNATIONAL JOURNAL OF PSYCHOLOGY, 2006, 41 (4), 276–281

Moral face and social face: Contingent self-esteem in Confucian society

Kwang-Kuo Hwang

National Taiwan University, Taipei, Taiwan

*T*hree empirical studies related to the Chinese concept of face are reviewed to provide examples of the indigenous approach of Chinese psychology. Using the technique of paired comparison, the first study indicated that college students (who are preparing to enter the job market) feel that they "have face" most when they do well in their academic performance, followed by being morally upright. Retirees (who have withdrawn from the workplace) feel that they "have face" most when their children are morally upright and successful in their careers. The second study (on patterns of emotional reactions of related others to an agent's social and moral incidents) showed, first, that incidents of positive achievement were generally evaluated by college students as being experienced with a more intense feeling of having face than were incidents of positive morality, while incidents of negative morality were experienced with a more intense feeling of "having no face" than were incidents of negative achievement. Second, for a positive incident of having face, the intensity of emotional reaction experienced by acquaintances was generally lower than that of family members. The difference was not so strong as in the negative incident of having no face. The third study (which was a cross-cultural one on cognitive distortion caused by misconduct of related others) indicated that American college students tended to adopt a consistent standard to judge the wrongness of illegal behaviours, regardless of their relationships with the transgressor. But Taiwanese college students tended to judge an illegal behaviour as more wrong when it was done by a person outside the family, while they held a more lenient attitude towards the misconduct of parents, and a similar or more harsh attitude towards their children. Research findings are interpreted in the context of Confucian tradition.

*T*rois études empiriques reliées au concept chinois de face (défini comme le statut atteint par un individu à travers la reconnaissance sociale de sa performance et de son sens moral) sont examinées afin d'illustrer l'approche indigène de la psychologie chinoise. La première étude a utilisé la technique de la comparaison pairée. Elle a montré que les étudiants collégiens (qui se préparent à entrer sur le marché du travail) sentent surtout qu'ils ont la face quand ils réussissent bien sur le plan académique, suivi par le fait d'être moralement honnête. Les retraités (ceux qui ont quitté leur travail) sentent surtout qu'ils ont la face quand leurs enfants sont moralement honnêtes et ont du succès dans leur carrière. La seconde étude fut effectuée sur les patrons de réactions émotionnelles des personnes proches par rapport à des agents d'événements sociaux et moraux. Elle a montré que les événements de réussite positive étaient généralement évalués par les étudiants collégiens comme étant vécus avec un sentiment plus intense d'avoir la face comparativement aux événements de moralité positive. En contrepartie, les événements de moralité négative étaient vécus avec un sentiment plus intense de ne pas avoir la face comparativement aux événements de réussite négative. En outre, pour un événement positif d'avoir la face, l'intensité de la réaction émotionnelle vécue par les connaissances était généralement plus faible que celle des membres de la famille. La différence n'était pas aussi forte que pour l'événement négatif de ne pas avoir la face. La troisième étude était une étude transculturelle sur la distorsion cognitive causée par la mauvaise conduite de personnes proches. Elle a indiqué que les étudiants collégiaux américains tendaient à adopter un standard logique pour juger l'inexactitude des comportements illégaux, sans tenir compte de leurs relations avec le transgresseur. Mais, les étudiants collégiaux taïwanais tendaient à juger un comportement illégal comme plus incorrect quand il était perpétré par une personne ne faisant pas partie de la famille, tandis qu'ils tenaient une attitude plus indulgente envers les mauvaises conduites de parents ainsi qu'une attitude similaire ou plus sévère envers leurs enfants. Les résultats de recherche sont interprétés dans le contexte de la tradition confucéenne.

Correspondence should be addressed to K.-K. Hwang, Rm 205, South Building, Department of Psychology, National Taiwan University, 1 Roosevelt Road, Sec. 4, Taipei, Taiwan, 106 ROC (E-mail: kkhwang@ntu.edu.tw).

This paper was written with the support of a grant from National Science Council, Republic of China, NSC 93-2752-H-002-001-PAE.

DOI: 10.1080/00207590544000040

S e revisaron tres estudios empíricos relacionados con el concepto de rostro en China como ejemplos del método de la psicología clínica tradicional. Aplicando la técnica de comparación apareada, el primer estudio encontró que la mayor parte de los estudiantes de licenciatura (quienes están preparándose para entrar al mercado laboral) sienten que "tienen un rostro" cuando tienen un buen rendimiento académico, lo cual los hace sentirse moralmente bien. La mayor parte de los pensionados (quienes han dejado de ir al sitio de trabajo) sienten que "tienen un rostro" cuando sus hijos se sienten moralmente bien y tienen éxito en sus carreras. El segundo estudio (sobre los patrones de reacciones emocionales de las personas relacionadas ante los incidentes sociales y morales de un agente) demostró que los estudiantes de licenciatura experimentaban los incidentes de logros positivos con una sensación más intensa de tener rostro que los incidentes de moralidad positiva, mientras que los incidentes de moralidad negativa eran experimentados con una sensación más intensa de "no tener rostro" que los incidentes de logros negativos. En segundo lugar, para un incidente positivo de "tener rostro", la intensidad de la reacción emocional experimentada por los conocidos era, por lo general, menor que la de los familiares. La diferencia no era tan fuerte como en el caso del incidente negativo de no tener rostro. El tercer estudio (un estudio transcultural sobre la distorsión cognitiva causada por la conducta inapropiada de los demás) encontró que los estudiantes de universidades de los Estados Unidos tendían a adoptar una norma consistente para juzgar lo incorrecto de las conductas ilegales, sin importar las relaciones que establecieran con el transgresor. Sin embargo, los estudiantes universitarios de Tasmania tendían a considerar incorrecta una conducta ilegal cuando se trataba de una persona ajena a la familia, y tenían una actitud más laxa hacia los problemas de comportamiento de los padres, y una actitud similar o más ruda hacia los hijos. Los resultados experimentales se interpretan en función del contexto de la tradición confuciana.

In Western social psychology, "face" is conceptualized as an individual's situated identity, or identity in a particular situation (Alexander & Rudd, 1981). In Confucian culture, face can be defined as an individual's contingent self-esteem (Ng, 2001), or as a person's cognitive response to social evaluation of his conduct in a particular situation. Face may have impact on a person's emotional state, or urge a person to take action to restore face. In any culture, an individual may experience a feeling of having or losing face because of positive or negative social evaluation (e.g., Goffman, 1959; Ting-Toomey, 1994), although face has special connotations in Chinese society (Ho, 1976; Hu, 1944; Hwang, 1987; Stover, 1974); this can be illuminated in the context of Confucian relationalism.

This article presents findings of several empirical studies on Chinese face. It is expected that the specific features of Chinese social behaviour can be illustrated by (1) social incidents that induce a feeling of having face or losing face, (2) the emotional reactions of related others to one's social incidents, and (3) one's cognitive distortion caused by misconduct of related others that may make one lose face.

MORAL FACE AND SOCIAL FACE

In Chinese society, there are clearly two types of face: social face and moral face (Cheng, 1986; Hu, 1944). Social face is gained either through the status achieved by one's talent, endeavours, or ability; or through the status ascribed by one's consanguineous relationships. Moral face refers to the social evaluation of one's moral character, which is the baseline of one's integrity of personality. An individual may choose not to strive for social face, but must protect moral face in all situations.

Based on these propositions, it might be expected that the importance of social face for college students and retired people might differ. College students are preparing to enter the job market to pursue career success, so they tend to value the social face achieved through academic performance. Retirees have withdrawn from the workplace. They may no longer care about their own career performance, but may experience the feeling of having or losing face through the achievements of their family members, especially their children. Nevertheless, both college students and retirees should care about their own moral face.

Based on such reasoning, Su and Hwang (2003) used a paired comparison technique with 56 retirees and 54 college students to examine the extent of the feeling of "having face" arising from the moral or academic (or career) performance of themselves, their children (or parents), or their friends. The same method was used to compare the extent of the feeling of "losing face" experienced when their own (or their family member's or friend's) immoral conduct or academic (or career) failure was exposed in public. The scores of original means were calculated by using the paired comparison method (Thurstone, 1927). The numerical values represent the extent of having or losing face for various incidents experienced by the participants.

Social incidents of having face

The first two incidents that make retirees most feel they "have face" are when their children are morally upright (0.719) and successful in their careers (0.647). The next two incidents pertain to their own performance (0.495; −0.004); and the last two relate to their friends (−0.686; −1.116).

Results show that the order of the first two pairs for college students is opposite to that of retirees. Because college students hope to enter the job market soon, they most feel they "have face" when they do well in their academic performance (1.312), followed by being morally upright (1.231). Next in importance is when their parents are morally upright (0.151) and successful in their careers (−0.087), and last is when their friends are morally upright (−1.026) and have a good academic performance (−1.581).

In comparing the data of retirees with that of college students, several points should be noted. First, the distribution of incidents on the similarity scale for paired comparisons made by retirees is more concentrated than that made by college students, implying that college students are able to make more distinct cognitive differentiations between the incidents than retirees. Second, being morally upright conveys more face than academic or career performance for all agents, except college students, who indicated that their academic performance (1.312) is relatively more important than being morally upright (1.231), although the difference is not significant. The data reflect an important fact about Chinese face: In general, moral face is more basic and important to most people than social face earned through the achievements of oneself or one's family (Cheng, 1986).

Third, one's own achievement and moral performance may make college students feel that they have more face than their parents, which reflects an individual orientation. In contrast, retirees have face more from their children's moral performance and academic achievements than from their own, which reflects a social (Yang, 1981) or relational orientation (Ho, 1991; Hwang, 2001). In other words, "individual orientation" or "social orientation" should be regarded as patterns of behaviour that might be elicited by a particular situational context, rather than a stable personality orientation or national character.

Social incidents of losing face

Moral face is the baseline for being an upright person, which should not be lost in any situation. Once it is lost, it is very hard for an individual to maintain a position in the community.

Results show that the incident that caused retirees the most serious feeling of losing face was personal moral deficiency (1.698). The next most serious was the moral deficiency of their son or daughter (1.229), personal career failure (0.54), and then failure of their son or daughter (0.508). Moral deficiency (−1.055) or career failure (−2.924) of a friend ranked lowest. The whole sequence reflects the differential structure of Chinese relationalism: Individuals tend to maintain psychosocial homeostasis by arranging interpersonal relationships with others from intimate to remote (Fei, 1948; Hsu, 1971; Hwang, 2000, 2001).

Though the mean scores reflecting the extent of losing face for various incidents were different for college students and retirees, the sequence was similar. The only exception was for college students, where the moral deficiency of a friend (−0.108) brought a stronger feeling of losing face than the career failure of parents (−1.509). When a college student has a friend with a moral deficiency, s/he might be treated similarly to the friend, or even be similarly accused by others. But if a friend has poor academic performance, an individual might feel enhanced face through downward social comparison. Thus, this incident ranked lowest in the extent of making a college student feel the loss of face (−2.837).

RELATIONALISM AND EMOTIONAL REACTION

Because college students are preparing to pursue careers, academic achievement is more important than being morally upright, and social face is more important than moral face in terms of the feeling of having face. However, moral face is the baseline of the integrity of personality. Although an individual may not strive for it, he should be careful not to lose it in any situation. Moral face is more important than social in terms of losing face.

In Confucian culture, when an individual violates a moral rule, a person's reaction may depend on that person's relationship with the agent. Liu (2002) asked 278 university students (150 men and 128 women) in Taiwan to read four scenarios about incidents of achievement or morality. The agent in the positive moral scenario helped a woman who fainted on the street to go to the hospital and saved her life. The agent in the positive achievement scenario was a student who had failed the Joint Entrance Examination for admission to a university, but he eventually passed the examination through hard work. The agent in the negative moral scenario was caught stealing from a store by the police. The agent in the negative achievement scenario dropped out of school due to poor grades. Participants were asked to evaluate the emotional reactions of people of different role relationships with the agent on a 7-point scale. The mean scores for emotional reactions were then calculated.

Figures 1 and 2 present the emotional reactions of "having face" and "having no face" as evaluated by the participants for each role. Two remarkable points should be noted: First, as predicted, incidents of positive achievement were generally evaluated by college students to be experienced with a more intense feeling of having face than incidents of positive morality (see Figure 1). Incidents of negative morality were experienced with a more intense feeling of "having no face" than incidents of negative achievement (see Figure 2). Second, for a positive incident of

having face, the intensity of emotional reaction experienced by acquaintances (including good friends, classmates, and teachers) was generally lower than that of family members. The difference was not so drastic as in the negative incident of having no face.

In other words, participants believed that acquaintances and family members might experience a similar intensity of face for one's positive incidents. When an individual suffers from a negative incident of having no face, family members may also experience a feeling of having no face, but acquaintances may sever relationships and thus will not experience a similar feeling of having no face. The pattern of emotional reactions reflects the Chinese conceptualization of family as a whole body sharing the experience of having face or losing the face. While one's acquaintances may share positive incidents, they do not seem to share the negative ones.

COGNITIVE DISTORTION

Because family members are perceived as parts of a body, if any one member of the family does

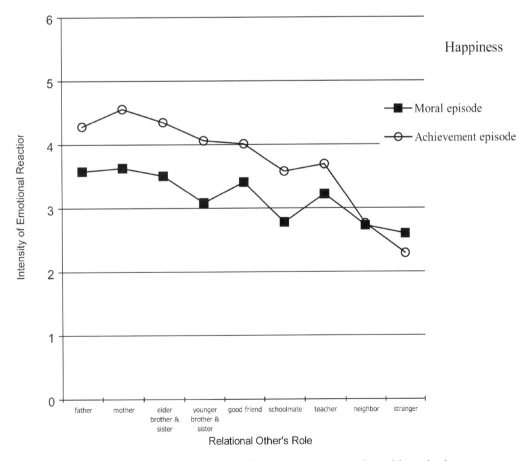

Figure 1. Relational other's emotional reaction to agent's positive episode.

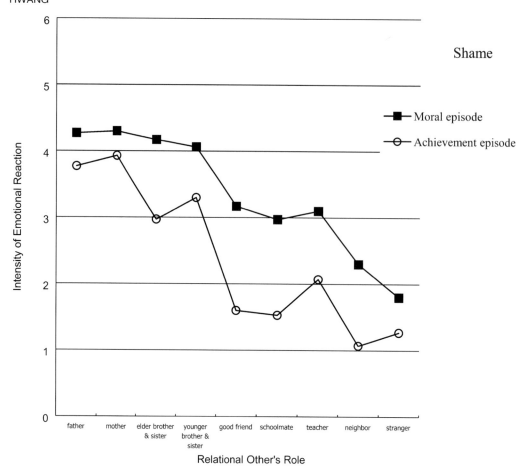

Figure 2. Relational other's emotional reaction to agent's negative episode.

something immoral, all family members may suffer from loss of face. Such a feeling may have an impact on one's moral judgment and result in cognitive distortion, which may reflect specific features of Confucian ethics and can be illustrated with a cross-cultural study on moral judgment between Taiwanese and American college students (Wei & Hwang, 1998).

In the second part of their study, 194 Taiwanese and American college students were asked to evaluate the extent of wrongness involved when a person violates negative duties towards different social targets. Responses to 20 items were subjected to factor analysis and three factors were obtained.

Factor 1 was labelled Violating the Social Norm and entailed behaviours that either destroy the social order or are prohibited by the law. It consisted of six items including "giving a gift to bribe someone or being bribed," "trying to be first and not standing in a queue," "tax evasion," "using insider information to make a profit in the stock market," "littering," and "maltreating one's child."

American subjects evaluated all behaviours described by the items of this factor as having a higher degree of wrongness than did Chinese subjects, no matter who the transgressor was (see Figure 3). American participants gave the different social targets only minor differences in scores, while Taiwanese allocated scores that increased as a function of the remoteness of the relationship with the transgressor. In other words, American college students tended to adopt a consistent standard to judge the wrongness of illegal behaviours, regardless of their relationships with the transgressor. However, Taiwanese college students tended to judge an illegal behaviour as being more wrong when it was done by a person outside the family, while they held a more lenient attitude towards the misconduct of parents (for the sake of protecting their face), and a similar or more harsh attitude towards their children (a necessity of disciplining them).

CONCLUSION

Concern about public image might be universal to people in various cultures, but the specific features of Chinese social behaviour related to face should

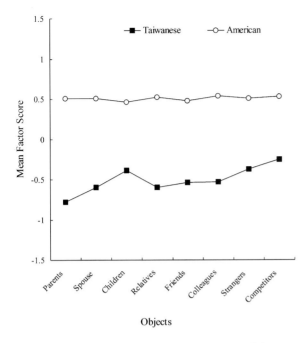

Figure 3. Factor scores on "violating law" by Taiwanese and American students.

be understood in the context of Confucian cultural traditions. It is expected that the empirical studies reviewed in this article, in combination with the theoretical modes of Confucian relationalism (Hwang, 2000, 2001), may help the reader to understand the indigenous approach of Chinese psychology.

REFERENCES

Alexander, C. N., & Rudd, J. (1981). Situated identities and response variables. In J. T. Tedeschi (Ed.), *Impression management theory and social psychological research* (pp. 83–103). New York: Academic Press.

Cheng, C. Y. (1986). The concept of face and its Confucian roots. *Journal of Chinese Philosophy, 13,* 329–348.

Fei, S. T. (1948). *Rural China*. [in Chinese]. Shanghai: Observer.

Goffman, E. (1959). *The presentation of self in everyday life.* New York: Doubleday, Anchor.

Ho, D. Y. F. (1976). On the concept of face. *American Journal of Sociology, 81,* 867–884.

Ho, D. Y. F. (1991). Relational orientation and methodological relationalism. *Bulletin of the Hong Kong Psychological Society, 26–27,* 81–95.

Hsu, F. L. K. (1971). Psychological homeostasis and *ren*: Conceptual tools for advancing psychological anthropology. *American Anthropologist, 73,* 23–44.

Hu, H. C. (1944). The Chinese concepts of "face". *American Anthropologist, 46,* 45–64.

Hwang, K. K. (1987). Face and favor: The Chinese power game. *American Journal of Sociology, 92,* 944–974.

Hwang, K. K. (2000). Chinese relationalism: Theoretical construction and methodological considerations. *Journal for the Theory of Social Behavior, 30,* 155–178.

Hwang, K. K. (2001). The deep structure of confucianism: A social psychological approach. *Asian Philosophy, 11,* 179–204.

Liu, D. W. (2002). *Relational others' emotional reactions to negative episodes of agency evaluated by college students in Taiwan.* Unpublished master thesis, National Taiwan University, Taiwan.

Ng, A. K. (2001). *Why Asians are less creative than Westerners.* Singapore: Prentice-Hall.

Stover, L. E. (1974). *The cultural ecology of Chinese civilization.* New York: Pica Press.

Su, S. Y., & Hwang, K. K. (2003). Face and relation in different domains of life: A comparision between senior citizens and university students. *Chinese Journal of Psychology, 45,* 295–311.

Thurstone, L. L. (1927). A law of comparative judgment. *Psychological Review, 34,* 273–286.

Ting-Toomey, S. (1994). *The challenge of facework: Cross-cultural and interpersonal issues.* New York: State University of New York Press.

Wei, C. F., & Hwang, K. K. (1998). Positive duties and negative duties: A cross-cultural comparison of moral judgment between Taiwanese and American college students. *Chinese Journal of Psychology, 40,* 137–153.

Yang, K. S. (1981). Social orientation and individual modernity among Chinese students in Taiwan. *Journal of Social Psychology, 113,* 159–170.

INTERNATIONAL JOURNAL OF PSYCHOLOGY, 2006, 41 (4), 282–286

Shufa: Chinese calligraphic handwriting (CCH) for health and behavioural therapy

Henry S. R. Kao

Department of Psychology, Sun Yat-Sen University, Guangzhou, China

*T*his paper presents an overview of psychological research on the Chinese art of calligraphy (*Shufa*). Using a theoretical framework, we have investigated the scientific nature of calligraphic brush handwriting as well as its treatment effects on behavioural and clinical disorders. The paper begins with an introduction to Chinese calligraphy, Chinese characters, and the character structures. This is followed by an account of a research-based framework of the psychological characteristics of Chinese calligraphy handwriting (CCH). Our basic research includes measures of the writer's physiological changes associated with the brush-writing act, and the results show that the practitioner experiences relaxation and emotional calmness evident in decelerated respiration, slower heart-rate, decreased blood pressure, and reduced muscular tension. The cognitive effects of the CCH practice included quickened response time and improved performance in discrimination and figure identification, as well as enhanced visual spatial abilities, spatial relations, abstract reasoning, and aspects of memory and attention in the practitioners. Following these findings, our applied and clinical research has resulted in positive effects of the CCH treatment on behavioural changes in individuals with autism, Attention Deficit Disorder (ADD), and Attention Deficit Hyperactivity Disorder (ADHD); on cognitive improvements in reasoning, judgement, and cognitive facilitation; and on hand steadiness in children with mild retardation; as well as enhanced memory, concentration, spatial orientation, and motor coordination in Alzheimer's patients. Similarly, we have successfully applied the CCH treatment to patients with psychosomatic diseases of hypertension and diabetes, as well as mental diseases of schizophrenia, depression, and neurosis in terms of the patients' emotions, concentration, and hospital behaviours. This new system of CCH behavioural treatment has also been applied to users of other writing systems. In summary, the present CCH research has its roots in a Chinese art, has been scientifically investigated, and offers an alternative approach to improved health.

*C*et article présente une vue d'ensemble de la recherche en psychologie sur l'art chinois de la calligraphie (*Shufa*). Utilisant un cadre de référence théorique, nous avons examiné la nature scientifique de l'écriture calligraphique au pinceau ainsi que ses effets thérapeutiques sur les troubles comportementaux et cliniques. L'article commence par une introduction de la calligraphie chinoise, des caractères chinois et de la structure des caractères. Ceci est suivi par un exposé du cadre de travail basé sur la recherche sur les caractéristiques psychologiques de l'écriture calligraphique chinoise (ECC). Notre recherche de base inclut des mesures des changements psychologiques chez les personnes pratiquant cet art. Les résultats montrent que ces personnes vivent une relaxation et un calme émotionnel qui sont mis en évidence par une respiration décélérée, des pulsations cardiaques plus lentes, une pression artérielle diminuée et une tension musculaire réduite. Les effets cognitifs de la pratique de l'ECC incluaient un temps de réponse plus rapide, une amélioration de la performance pour la discrimination et l'identification d'une figure et une amélioration sur le plan des habiletés visuo-spatiales, des relations spatiales, du raisonnement abstrait et d'aspects de la mémoire et de l'attention. Suivant ces données, notre recherche appliquée et clinique utilisant un traitement avec ECC nous a permis d'obtenir des effets positifs sur plusieurs plans : des changements comportementaux chez des personnes autistes, des personnes avec trouble de déficit de l'attention et des personnes avec trouble de déficit de l'attention avec hyperactivité; des améliorations cognitives dans le raisonnement, le jugement et la facilitation cognitive et plus d'habiletés manuelles chez des enfants ayant un retard intellectuel moyen; ainsi qu'une amélioration de la mémoire, de la concentration, de l'orientation spatiale et de la coordination motrice chez des patients ayant l'Alzheimer. Similairement, nous avons appliqué avec succès le traitement avec ECC auprès de patients souffrant de maladies psychosomatiques

Correspondence should be addressed to Henry S. R. Kao, Research Professor, Department of Psychology, Sun Yat-Sen University, Guangzhou, China. (E-mail: hrnyksr@hkucc.hku.hk)

Preparation of this paper was supported by a grant (NSC 92-2416-H-008-030) from the National Science Council, Taiwan, while the author was with the Institute of Human Resource Management, National Central University, Taiwan.

DOI: 10.1080/00207590544000059

d'hypertension et de diabète et auprès de patients ayant des maladies mentales comme la schizophrénie, la dépression et la névrose. Chez ces patients, les effets se sont faits sentir sur le plan des émotions, de la concentration et des comportements à l'hôpital. Ce nouveau système de l'ECC en tant que traitement comportemental fut aussi appliqué auprès d'utilisateurs d'autres systèmes d'écriture. En somme, la présente recherche sur l'ECC prend racine dans un art chinois, a été étudiée scientifiquement et offre une approche alternative de traitement pour améliorer la santé.

*E*ste artículo presenta una visión de conjunto de la investigación en psicología sobre el arte de la caligrafía china (*Shufa*). Utilizando un marco de referencia teórico, hemos investigado la naturaleza científica de la escritura caligráfica al pincel, así como los efectos terapéuticos de la misma sobre los trastornos clínicos y del comportamiento. El artículo inicia con una introducción a la caligrafía china, los caracteres chinos y la estructura de los caracteres. En seguida se presenta una explicación sobre el esquema experimental de las características psicológicas de la escritura caligráfica china (ECC). Nuestra investigación básica incluye la medición de los cambios psicológicos en las personas que practican este arte. Los resultados muestran que estas personas experimentan un estado de relajación y una calma emocional que se manifiestan como una respiración desacelerada, pulsaciones cardíacas más lentas, una reducción en la presión arterial y una disminución en la tensión muscular. Los efectos cognitivos de la ECC incluían un menor tiempo de respuesta, una mayor discriminación e identificación de figuras, y también una mejora en las habilidades espaciales, en las relaciones espaciales, en el razonamiento abstracto y en aspectos diversos de la memoria y la atención de quienes la practicaban. Después de estos resultados, nuestras investigaciones clínicas y aplicadas han generado efectos positivos en cuanto al uso de un tratamiento mediante la ECC, al aplicarla a cambios conductuales en el autismo, en el trastorno por déficit de atención (TDA) y en el trastorno por déficit de atención e hiperactividad (TDAH), mejoras cognitivas en el razonamiento, en el juicio y en la facilitación cognitiva y mayores habilidades manuales en aquellos niños que presentan un retardo intelectual leve, además de un mejoramiento en la memoria, la concentración, la orientación espacial y la coordinación motriz en pacientes con Alzheimer. Asimismo, hemos aplicado exitosamente el tratamiento con la ECC en pacientes con padecimientos psicosomáticos, hipertensión y diabetes, y también con enfermedades mentales como la esquizofrenia, la depresión y la neurosis, pacientes en quienes los efectos se hacen sentir en el plano de las emociones, la concentración y los comportamientos en el hospital. Este nuevo sistema con la ECC como tratamiento conductual también se ha aplicado a personas que practican otros sistemas de escritura. En suma, la presente investigación sobre la ECC tiene sus raíces en un arte proveniente de China, ha sido estudiada con el método científico y representa un método alternativo de tratamiento para mejorar la salud.

INTRODUCTION

Shufa or Chinese calligraphy is the writing of Chinese characters by hand using a soft-tipped brush; it has been used historically as a means of communication. The study of Chinese calligraphy in the past has focused mainly on how to execute and appreciate it artistically by following the experiences of the great masters. In the last three decades, we have investigated the psychological processes of Chinese brush handwriting from several dimensions of psychology.

Chinese characters and the characters' structuring

Chinese brush handwriting involves a process of visual spatial structuring of the elements of the characters. They are written within an imaginary, subdivided square in which the execution of its strokes, the shaping, and the spacing and framing of the character occur. The formation of a character involves inscribing and aligning its strokes according to the patterns of the established character (Billeter, 1990).

The calligraphic writing act involves one's bodily functions as well as one's cognitive activities. Motor control and manoeuvring of the brush follow the character configurations. There is, therefore, an integration of the mind, body, and character interwoven in a dynamic graphonomic process (Kao, 2000).

The organization of the character entails certain geometric properties, including the topological principles of connectivity, closure, orientation, and symmetry, etc. In writing, these properties cause the writer's perceptual, cognitive, and bodily conditions to engage in corresponding adjustments and representations (L. Chen, 1982; Kao, 2000).

PSYCHOLOGICAL ASPECTS OF BRUSH CHARACTER WRITING

A research-based general framework has been advanced to highlight the act of brush character writing in any language.

1. The writer's perceptual, cognitive, and motor activities are feedback regulated and are integrated in a dynamic writing task with the writer's body interfacing the character in an interactive process. The visual-spatial properties of the character affect the cognitive and motor activities of the writer during writing (Kao, 1973, 1976; Kao, Smith, & Knutson, 1969).

2. The body–character interlocking involves a projection by the writer of the character configurations in close correspondence and parallel to the body's changing physical orientations. In this interface, someone's visual-spatial patterns of the character are varied and more prominently featured than others, and would contribute to the differential complexity of the writing tasks (Kao, Shek, & Lee, 1983).

3. The body, as the reference for the writing act, initiates motion according to the geometry of the character and generates the corresponding patterns of the writing movements. Since all scripts share certain geometric properties in their construction, the basic principles of drawing and handwriting for Chinese are common between Chinese and English, e.g., the motor control variability in the writing act. This commonality makes possible the generality of findings from researching Chinese handwriting to alphabetic and other scripts (Kao, 1983; Kao & Wong, 1988; Wong & Kao, 1991).

4. Because of the softness of the brush tip, the CCH act involves a 3-D motion, which generates a powerful source of impact on the practitioner's perceptual, cognitive, and physiological changes during its practice. This impact also varies according to the modes of handwriting control, i.e., tracing, copying, and freehand (Shek, Kao, & Chau, 1986).

5. In character formation, the brush is manoeuvred to produce 2-D strokes, varying in size, form, and direction. The task of the writer is to move the brush to track the established stroke patterns from memory or copybooks. This act resembles a driver's steering of a car by using its front wheels as cursors in tracking the spatial displacement of the vehicle relative to the road (Kao & Smith, 1969). The cursors in CCH tracking take the form of the brush tip.

6. A square is the perfect geometric pattern incorporating such features as hole, linearity, symmetry, parallelism, connectivity, and orientation. A Chinese character portrays an imaginary square. With an implied correspondence between the square and the character, a character may vary in terms of its geometric properties. These inherent properties contribute to the differential cognitive effects during character reading and writing (X. F. Chen & Kao, 2002; Kao, 2000; Kao & Chen, 2000).

7. Psychophysiological changes associated with CCH writing include heart-rate, respiration, blood pressure, digital pulse volume, EMG, EEG, skin conductance, skin temperature, etc. (Kao, Lam, Robinson, & Yen, 1989).

8. Cognitive changes associated with CCH practice include such abilities as clerical speed and accuracy, spatial ability, abstract reasoning, digit span, short-term memory, picture memory, and cognitive reaction time (Kao, 1992a). These changes are varied and affected by the whole motor programme as well as the subprogrammes of the components of the character (Chau, Kao, & Shek, 1986).

9. Stylistic variations of written characters reflect the individualised forms and organization of the strokes of the character. Chinese characters executed in different calligraphic styles and orthographic forms would lead to variations in the writer's behavioural responses (Kao, Mak, & Lam, 1986a).

BASIC RESEARCH

A host of experiments measured a writer's physiological changes associated with the practice of CCH. Common results indicate that subjects experienced relaxation and emotional calmness throughout this writing act. Their respiration rate decelerated, heart-rate slowed down, and blood pressure decreased, and digital pulse volume increased with corresponding reduction in EMG (Kao et al., 1989). The heart-rate can also differentiate different modes of handwriting control (Kao & Shek, 1986). Moreover, the practitioner's EEG activities in the right hemisphere were found to be significantly greater than those in the left hemisphere during such writing (Kao, Shek, Chau, & Lam, 1986b).

For the post-task cognitive effects of the CCH, the subjects performed better in figure identification and form discrimination tasks. A second study showed a significant reaction time reduction in both hemispheres for subjects with calligraphy experience (Gao, 1994). A third study further disclosed that the right hemisphere reaction time reduction was more distinct for experienced calligraphers than the novices (Guo & Kao, 1991).

Further, a series of experiments has shown that the CCH practice improves abilities in visual attention, spatial ability, perceptual speed and accuracy, spatial relations, abstract reasoning, as well as in response facilitation, short-term memory, and pictorial memory (Kao, 1992b; Kao, Gao, Wang, Cheung, & Chiu, 2000c). In addition, preliminary post-task ERP data disclosed a significant increase of cortical activation in the experimental subjects, but not in the controls (Kao, Gao, Miao, & Liu, 2004).

APPLIED AND CLINICAL RESEARCH

As for behavioural changes, children with Autism, Attention Deficiency Disorder (ADD), and Attention-Deficit/Hyperactivity Disorder (ADHD) have benefited from the CCH training. The improvements include the ADHD children's attention and social communication (Kao, Chen, & Chang, 1997) as well as the autistic children's negative behaviour and communication in the family or schools (Kao, Lai, Fok, Gao, & Ma, 2000e).

Some CCH cognitive treatments have been conducted. In the case of mild retardation, the treatment resulted in increased visual attention, reasoning, judgement, and cognitive speed and accuracy as well as hand steadiness and control precision (Kao, Hu, & Zhang, 2000d). For the Alzheimer's patients, the treatment improved their short-term memory, concentration, and temporal and spatial orientation, as well as motor coordination. The normal elderly also improved in their spatial ability and pictorial memory (Kao, 2003; Kao & Gao, 2000; Kao et al., 2000c).

For psychosomatic diseases, we started with patients suffering from essential hypertension (Guo, Kao, & Liu, 2001). After the CCH practice, their systolic and diastolic blood pressures showed a significant reduction. A related study reported a reduction of anxiety and an increase of alpha waves, as well as a decrease of heart-rate after the CCH training (Kao, Guo, & Liu, 2001). Further, stress-related conditions of the diabetes II patients and business executives exhibited a post-CCH reduction in states of anxiety and moods (Goan, Ng, & Kao, 2000; Kao, Ding, & Cheng, 2000a).

Finally, we also examined the CCH treatment effects on mental and stroke patients. After a 3-month training schedule, the schizophrenic patients improved significantly in their positive hospital behaviours as well as their negative symptoms, while the control patients made no improvement (Fan, Kao,Wang, & Guo, 1999). In separate study with a 2-week CCH treatment protocol, the stroke patients made significant improvements in their palm strength and fine motor coordination (Chiu, Kao, & Ho, 2002).

CONCLUSIONS

This paper has presented an overview of our research on Chinese calligraphic handwriting. These varied findings are founded on a theoretical formulation, on associated basic research, and on varied applications. As for the reasons behind all these positive effects of the practice of CCH, two views are offered. First, the act of brushing causes heightened attention and concentration on the part of practitioners and results in their physiological slowdown and relaxation, causing the subsequent changes in their emotions. Second, concurrent to these states, some cognitive effects occur in relation to a person's attention and concentration as a function of the geometric characteristics of the writing script, which contribute to the facilitative benefits observed in one's cognitive activities.

We are currently developing our CCH treatment system for broader applications to cover English alphabets and Japanese and Korean scripts, with some success. We are optimistic that this new therapeutic system will be helpful not only to users of the Chinese script, but also to users of other writing systems.

REFERENCES

Billeter, J. F. (1990). *Chinese art of writing* (pp. 27–44). New York: Rizzoli.

Chau, A. W. L., Kao, H. S. R., & Shek, D. T. L. (1986). Writing time of double-character Chinese words: Effects of interrupting writing responses. In H. S. R. Kao, G. P. van Galen & R. Hoosain (Eds.), *Graphonomics: Contemporary research in handwriting* (pp. 273–288). Amsterdam: North-Holland.

Chen, L. (1982). Topological structure in visual perception. *Science, 218,* 699–700.

Chen, X. F., & Kao, H. S. R. (2002). Visual spatial properties and orthographic processing of Chinese characters. In H. S. R. Kao, C. K. Leong & D. G. Gao (Eds.), *Cognitive and neuroscience studies of Chinese language* (pp. 175–194). Hong Kong: HKU Press.

Chiu, M. L., Kao, H. S. R., & Ho, S. M. Y. (2002). The efficacy of Chinese calligraphic handwriting on stroke patients: A multiple cases study. In A. D. Korczyn (Ed.), *Proceedings of the 2nd International Congress on Vascular Dementia.* Salzburg, Austria. Jan. 24–27, 2002.

Fan, Z. S., Kao, H. S. R., Wang, Y. L., & Guo, N. F. (1999). Calligraphic treatment of schizophrenic patients. In H. S. R. Kao (Ed.), *Chinese calligraphy therapy* (pp. 381–398). Hong Kong: HKU Press.

Gao, D. G. (1994). An exploratory research on the effects of Chinese calligraphic writing on brain reading times. In Q. Jing, H. Zhang, & D. Peng (Eds.), *Information processing of Chinese language* (pp. 191–199). Beijing: Beijing Normal University Press.

Goan, C. H., Ng, S. H., & Kao, H. S. R. (2000). Calligraphic practices and emotional states of managers and administrators. *International Journal of Behavioural Medicine, 7*, S1, 72.

Guo, K., & Kao, H. S. R. (1991). Effect of calligraphy writing on cognitive processing in the two hemispheres. In G. E. Stelmach (Ed.), *Motor control of handwriting: Proceedings of the 5th Biennial Conference of the International Graphonomics Society* (pp. 30–32), Tempe, Arizona, October 27–30, 1991.

Guo, N. F., Kao, H. S. R., & Liu, X. (2001). Calligraphy, hypertension and the type-A personality. *Annals of Behavioral Medicine, 23*, S2001, S159.

Kao, H. S. R. (1973). The effects of hand-finger exercise on human handwriting performance. *Ergonomics, 16*, 171–175.

Kao, H. S. R. (1976). On educational ergonomics. *Ergonomics, 19*, 667–681.

Kao, H. S. R. (1983). Progressive motion variability in handwriting tasks. *Acta Psychologica, 54*, 149–159.

Kao, H. S. R. (1992a). Psychological research on calligraphy. *International Journal of Psychology, 27*, 137.

Kao, H. S. R. (1992b). Effect of calligraphy writing on cognitive processing. *International Journal of Psychology, 27*, 138.

Kao, H. S. R. (Ed.). (2000). *Chinese calligraphy therapy* (pp. 3–42). Hong Kong: Hong Kong University Press.

Kao, H. S. R. (2003). Chinese calligraphic handwriting for health and rehabilitation of the elderly. *Book of Abstracts* (p. 68). Second World Congress of the International Society of Physical and Rehabilitation Medicine. Prague, May 18–22, 2003.

Kao, H. S. R., & Chen, X. (2000). Effect of geometric properties of Chinese script on visual processing. *International Journal of Psychology, 35*, 149.

Kao, H. S. R., Chen, C. C., & Chang, T. M. (1997). The effect of calligraphy practice on character recognition reaction time among children with ADHD disorder. In R. Roth (Ed.), *Psychologists facing the challenge of a global culture with human rights and mental health. Proceedings of the 55th Annual Convention of the Council of Psychologists* (pp. 45–49), Graz, Austria, July 14–18, 1997.

Kao, H. S. R., Ding, B. K., & Cheng, S. W. (2000a). Brush handwriting treatment of emotional problems in patients with Type II diabetes. *International Journal of Behavioural Medicine, 7*, S-1, 50.

Kao, H. S. R., & Gao, D. (2000). Effects of practising Chinese calligraphy on visual-spatial ability and pictorial memory in normal aged people. *International Journal of Psychology, 35*, 302.

Kao, H. S. R., Gao, D. G., Miao, D. M., & Liu, X. F. (2004). *Cognitive facilitation associated with Chinese brush handwriting: The case of symmetric and asymmetric characters.* Unpublished manuscript, Department of Psychology, University of Hong Kong, Hong Kong.

Kao, H. S. R., Gao, D., & Wang, M. (2000b). Brush handwriting treatment of cognitive deficiencies in Alzheimer's disease patients. *Neurobiology of Aging, 21*, 1S, 14.

Kao, H. S. R., Gao, D. G., Wang, M. Q., Cheung, H. Y., & Chiu, J. (2000c). Chinese calligraphic handwriting: Treatment of cognitive deficiencies of Alzheimer's disease patients. *Alzheimer's Reports, 3*, 281–287.

Kao, H. S. R., Guo, N. F., & Liu, X. (2001). Effects of calligraphy practice on EEG and blood pressure in hypertensive patients. *Annals of Behavioral Medicine, 23*, S085.

Kao, H. S. R., Hu, B., & Zhang (2000d). Effects of Chinese calligraphic handwriting on reasoning, executive abilities and psychological health of children with mild mental retardation. In H. S. R. Kao (Ed.), *Chinese calligraphy therapy* (pp. 321–344). Hong Kong: HKU Press.

Kao, H. S. R., Lai, S. F., Fok, W. Y., Gao, D. G., & Ma, T. H. (2000e). Brush handwriting treatment of negative behaviours in school and at home in children with autism. *Book of Abstracts, 8*. Glasgow, Autism-Europe Congress, May 19–21, 2000.

Kao, H. S. R., Lam, P. W., Robinson, L., & Yen, N. S. (1989). Psychophysiological changes associated with Chinese calligraphy. In P. Plamondon, C. Y. Suen, & M. L. Simner (Eds.), *Computer recognition and human production of handwriting* (pp. 349–381). Singapore: World Scientific Publishing.

Kao, H. S. R., Mak, P. H., & Lam, P. W. (1986a). Handwriting pressure: Effects of task complexity, control mode and orthographic differences. In H. S. R. Kao, G. P. van Galen, & R. Hoosain (Eds.), *Graphonomics: Contemporary research in handwriting* (pp. 47–66). Amsterdam: North-Holland.

Kao, H. S. R., & Shek, D. T. L. (1986). Modes of handwriting control in Chinese calligraphy: Some psychophysiological explorations. In H. S. R. Kao & R. Hoosain (Eds.), *Linguistics, psychology and the Chinese language* (pp. 317–333). Hong Kong: University of Hong Kong.

Kao, H. S. R., Shek, D. T. L., Chau, A. W. L., & Lam, P. W. (1986b). An exploratory study of the EEG activities accompanying Chinese calligraphy writing. In H. S. R. Kao & R. Hoosain (Eds.), *Linguistics, psychology and the Chinese language* (pp. 223–244). Hong Kong: University of Hong Kong.

Kao, H. S. R., Shek, D. T. L., & Lee, E. S. P. (1983). Control modes and task complexity in tracing and handwriting performance. *Acta Psychologica, 54*, 69–77.

Kao, H. S. R., & Smith, K. U. (1969). Cybernetic television methods applied to feedback analysis of automobile safety. *Nature, 222*, 299–300.

Kao, H. S. R., Smith, K. U., & Knutson, R. (1969). Experimental cybernetic analysis of handwriting and penpoint design. *Ergonomics, 12*, 453–458.

Kao, H. S. R., & Wong, C. M. (1988). Pen pressure in Chinese handwriting. *Perceptual and Motor Skills, 67*, 778.

Shek, D. T. L., Kao, H. S. R., & Chau, A. W. L. (1986). Attentional resources allocation process in different modes of handwriting control. In H. S. R. Kao, G. P. van Galen, & R. Hoosain (Eds.), *Graphonomics: Contemporary research in handwriting* (pp. 289–304). Amsterdam: North-Holland.

Wong, T. H., & Kao, H. S. R. (1991). Drawing principles in Chinese handwriting. In J. Wann, N. Sovik, & A. Wing (Eds.), *Development of graphic skills* (pp. 93–112). New York: Academic Press.

INTERNATIONAL JOURNAL OF PSYCHOLOGY, 2006, 41 (4), 287–292

Psychology Press
Taylor & Francis Group

Indigenous psychological analysis of academic achievement in Korea: The influence of self-efficacy, parents, and culture

Uichol Kim

Inha Fellow Professor, Inha University, Incheon, Korea

Young-Shin Park

Inha University, Incheon, Korea

*T*his paper examines the factors that contribute to the high educational achievement of Korean students. The authors outline the limitations of psychological and educational theories that emphasize the biological basis (i.e., innate ability, IQ), individualistic values (e.g., intrinsic motivation, ability attribution, and self-esteem), and structural features (e.g., high educational spending, small class size, and individualized instruction). Although the Korean government spends significantly less per student, class size is larger, cooperative learning is emphasized, and students have lower self-concepts, they outperform their Western counterparts in reading, mathematics, and sciences (National Center for Educational Statistics, 2000; Organization for Economic Co-operation and Development, 2003). The indigenous psychology approach is used to examine factors that explain the high academic achievement of Korean students. Empirical studies that examine the role of self-efficacy at the individual level, social support at the relational level, and Confucian values at the cultural level are reviewed. First, Koreans view education as a part of self-cultivation that is pursued for its own sake and as a way to achieve personal, social, and occupational success. Second, Koreans do not believe in innate ability but believe it can be acquired through persistent effort and discipline. Third, parents play a key role in maintaining a strong relational bond and influencing their children's achievement throughout their lives. The sacrifice and support provided by parents are essential ingredients for their children's success. Fourth, emotional support, rather than informational support, is reported to be the most important. Fifth, self-serving bias has not been found: Students attribute their success to effort and failure to a lack of effort and ability. Finally, although Western theories assume guilt and external pressure to have negative consequences, the reverse is the case. In Korea, children feel a sense of indebtedness toward their parents for all their devotion, sacrifice, and support. This promotes filial piety and academic achievement. Parental expectation and pressure had positive impact on their children's academic achievement.

*C*et article examine les facteurs qui contribuent à la forte réussite scolaire des étudiants coréens. Les auteurs soulignent les limites des théories en psychologie et en éducation qui mettent l'emphase sur les bases biologiques (c.-à-d. les habiletés innées et le QI), les valeurs individualistes (p. ex., la motivation intrinsèque, l'attribution d'habileté et l'estime de soi) et les caractéristiques de structure (p. ex., les dépenses élevées en éducation, les petits groupes classe et l'enseignement individualisé). Quoique le gouvernement coréen dépense significativement moins par étudiant, que les groupes classe soient plus grands, que l'emphase soit mise sur l'enseignement coopératif et que les étudiants aient un concept de soi plus faible, ces derniers obtiennent des performances supérieures à leurs homologues occidentaux en lecture, en mathématiques et en sciences (National Center for Educational Statistics, 2000; Organization for Economic Co-operation and Development, 2003). L'approche de la psychologie indigène est utilisée pour examiner les facteurs qui expliquent la forte réussite académique des étudiants coréens. Les études empiriques qui examinent le rôle de l'efficacité de soi au niveau de l'individu, le soutien social au niveau relationnel et les valeurs confucéennes au niveau culturel sont analysées. Premièrement, les Coréens voient l'éducation comme faisant partie de la culture personnelle qui est poursuivie pour son propre bien et comme une façon d'atteindre un succès personnel, social et professionnel. Deuxièmement, les Coréens ne croient à l'habileté innée, mais croient qu'il est possible de l'acquérir avec une

---

Correspondence should be addressed to Uichol Kim, Dept of Psychology, Chung-Ang University, 221 Huksuk-dong Dongjak-ku, Seoul, 156-756, Korea (e-mail: uicholk@chol.com).

This research was supported by the Chung-Ang University Special Research Grant in 1998.

DOI: 10.108000207590544000068

discipline et des efforts persistants. Troisièmement, les parents jouent un rôle clé dans le maintien de liens relationnels solides et influencent la réussite de leurs enfants tout au long de leur vie. Le sacrifice et le soutien des parents sont des ingrédients essentiels pour le succès de leurs enfants. Quatrièmement, il apparaît que le soutien émotionnel est plus important que le soutien informationnel. Cinquièmement, il ne semble pas y avoir de biais égocentrique: les étudiants attribuent leurs succès à leurs efforts et leurs échecs au manque d'effort et d'habilité. Finalement, quoique les théories occidentales prétendent que la culpabilité et les pressions extérieures ont des conséquences négatives, l'inverse est le cas. En Corée, les enfants ont un sentiment de dettes envers leurs parents pour leur dévotion, leur sacrifice et leur soutien. Cela promeut la piété filiale et la réussite académique. Les attentes et pressions parentales ont un impact positif sur la réussite académique de leurs enfants.

*E*ste artículo analiza los factores que contribuyen al alto rendimiento educativo de los estudiantes de Corea. Los autores subrayan las limitaciones de las teorías psicológicas y educativas que hacen énfasis en las bases biológicas (es decir, las habilidades innatas, el CI), en los valores individualistas (por ejemplo, la motivación intrínseca, la atribución de habilidades y la autoestima) y en las características estructurales (por ejemplo, las altas inversiones en educación, el tamaño pequeño de los grupos y la instrucción individualizada). Si bien el gobierno de Corea invierte significativamente menos por estudiante, el tamaño de los grupos es mayor, se subraya el aprendizaje cooperativo y los estudiantes tienen conceptos más bajos de sí mismos, muestran un rendimiento mucho mayor que sus contrapartes occidentales en la lectura, las matemáticas y las ciencias (National Center for Educational Statistics, 2000; Organization for Economic Co-operation and Development, 2003). El enfoque de la psicología tradicional se usa para revisar factores que explican el alto rendimiento académico de los estudiantes coreanos. Se revisan aquí los estudios empíricos que analizan el papel de la eficacia del yo a nivel individual, el apoyo social a nivel de relaciones y los valores confucianos a nivel cultural. En primer lugar, los coreanos ven la educación como parte de la cultura personal que persiguen para su propio bienestar y como un medio para alcanzar el éxito personal, social y laboral. En segundo lugar, los coreanos no creen en las habilidades innatas, pero creen que pueden ser adquiridas con esfuerzo y disciplina persistentes. En tercer lugar, los padres desempeñan un papel clave para mantener lazos sólidos en sus relaciones y para influir en los logros de sus hijos durante toda su vida. El sacrificio y el apoyo de los padres son ingredientes básicos para el éxito de los hijos. En cuarto lugar, el apoyo emocional parece ser el más importante, más que el apoyo en información. En quinto lugar, no parece haber una tendencia egocéntrica: los estudiantes atribuyen su éxito al esfuerzo y su fracaso a la falta de esfuerzo y de habilidades. Por último, aunque las teorías occidentales asumen que la culpa y la presión externa tienen consecuencias negativas, en realidad ocurre lo contrario. En Corea, los niños sienten que tienen una deuda hacia sus padres, por su devoción, su sacrificio y su apoyo. Esto promueve la piedad filial y el logro académico. Las expectativas y presiones de los padres tuvieron un impacto positivo sobre los logros académicos de sus hijos.

In 1960, South Korea (hereafter abbreviated as Korea) had all the problems of a resource-poor, low-income, illiterate, and under-developed country. The per capita GNP stood at $82 and the literacy and educational levels were among of the lowest in the world. During the past 40 years, the economy grew rapidly, with the per capita GNP increasing to $1640 in 1981 and to around $10,000 in 1997. This phenomenal economic growth has been spurred by educational transformations. Currently, the literacy rate is 98% and high school enrolment is 99%.

In international studies, Korean students are ranked near the top in knowledge, skill, and performance. They are ranked 2nd in mathematics and 5th in science among students from 39 countries (National Center for Educational Statistics, 2000). For comparison, students from the United States (abbreviated as US) are ranked 19th and 18th respectively. In a study of Grade 9 students in 31 countries, Korean students are ranked 1st in scientific literacy, 2nd in math

literacy, and 6th in reading literacy (Organization for Economic Co-operation and Development, 2003). Students from the US are ranked 14th, 19th, and 15th respectively. Traditional psychological and educational theories that emphasize biology (i.e., innate ability, IQ), individualistic values (e.g., intrinsic motivation, ability attribution, and self-esteem), and structural features (e.g., educational spending, small class size, and individualized instruction) have difficulty explaining the relatively poor performance of the US students and the high achievement of Korean students.

TRADITIONAL APPROACHES

Lewis Terman developed the Stanford-Binet IQ Test to measure native intelligence. He and his colleagues used the test to document individual, sex, ethnic, and racial differences and to shape some US policies (i.e., forced sterilization, segregation of races and sex, and restriction of immigration; Chorover, 1980). The IQ test was developed to fit ideological preconceptions and was not based on strict scientific criteria. For example, when the first version of the test was published in 1916, girls of all ages outscored boys by an average of 2–4%. Terman unilaterally deleted, revised, or added new items so that this difference disappeared and subsequently boys did better than girls (Kamin, 1974). In 1924, Asians were labelled as a "genetically inferior" race, and the US National Origins Act was passed to bar Asians from immigrating into the US (H. C. Kim, 1992).

Lynn and Vanhanen (2002) are currently proclaiming the same eugenic ideal, but with a different set of results. In their study of 60 nations, they have found that East Asians had the highest IQ: 106 for Korea, 105 for Japan, 104 for Taiwan, and 103 for Singapore. Europeans and Americans had lower scores: 98 for the US, 100 for the United Kingdom, and 102 for Germany. They conclude that the IQ scores reflect the racial superiority of East Asians. East Asians have now become a superior race due to their genes, although they were an inferior race 80 years ago! Moreover, the particular gene that is responsible for academic achievement has not been identified.

Traditional psychological and educational theories assume that the differences in academic performance can be explained by innate ability, personality, or environmental factors. However, Bandura (1997) found that academic achievement is mediated by the generative capability known as "self-efficacy." It is defined as "beliefs in one's capabilities to organize and execute the courses of action required to produce given attainments" (p. 3). When children and adults are matched for a specific ability (e.g., academic, athletic, or business skills), those with higher efficacy belief performed significantly better than those with lower efficacy belief. Students in the US, Europe, and Asia who had the self-efficacy beliefs to discipline themselves, to develop cognitive skills, and to obtain the necessary support from parents, teachers, and friends, performed well in school (Bandura, 1997; Park & Kim, 2004).

At the cultural level, the differences in academic achievement can be attributable to differences in values. Culture is defined as *the collective utilization of natural and human resources to achieve desired outcomes* (U. Kim, 2001). Differences in cultures exist because we have different goals, utilize different methods and resources to attain them, and attach different meanings to them. For example, when students were asked whether "enjoying life is more important than preparing

for life," 27% of US students *strongly agreed*, compared to 8% of Korean students (National Center for Educational Statistics, 2000). Second, when they were asked, "how much effort do you need to succeed in math," 8% of US students replied *a lot of effort*, compared to 36% of Korean students. Third, although the US students did poorly in math and science, they had high self-esteem: They are ranked 1st in self-concept for science and 4th in math. In contrast, Korean students had low self-esteem: they are ranked 32nd and 21st respectively. Fourth, Korean students who believed that they had to expend a lot of effort to do well in math had higher scores. Overall, Korean students did not believe that they were good and believed that they needed to work hard to do well. The US students believed that they were good and felt that moderate effort was enough, perhaps because many people in the US believe that expending a lot of effort means a lack of ability (Nicholls & Miller, 1984).

As for the motivation for studying math, 41% of US students *strongly agreed* that it is "to get the desired job," compared to 10% of Korean students (National Center for Educational Statistics, 2000). The vast majority of Korean students reported relational and social motivation: 85% agreed that it is to "enter a desired university" and 62% agreed that it is "to please their parents." For Korean students, relational and social motivations far outweighed personal motivation.

Finally, the US governmental spending per student is one of the highest in the world. It spends more than twice that spent in Korea (Organization for Economic Co-operation and Development, 2003). Also, the class size in the US is small so teachers can provide individualized instruction. In Korea, the class size is as large as 40 or 50 and the curriculum emphasizes cooperative learning. In spite of these structural benefits, US students perform significantly less well than Korean students.

INDIGENOUS PSYCHOLOGY

Indigenous psychology advocates examining knowledge, skills, and beliefs that people have about themselves, and studying them in their natural contexts. It represents a bottom-up approach and advocates a transactional paradigm (U. Kim, 2001). Epistemology, theories, concepts, and methods are developed to correspond with psychological phenomena. The goal is not to abandon science, objectivity, and a search for universals, but to create a science that is firmly grounded in the descriptive understanding. The goal is to create a more rigorous, systematic, universal science that can be theoretically and empirically verified. This approach is consistent with the sociocognitive theory advocated by Bandura (1997).

Cultural values, family, and self-cultivation in Korea

With the adoption of Confucianism about 2000 years ago, individuals of merit were selected through regional and national examinations. Successful candidates were given a position as a governmental official. In return for their services, they were given a large tract of land from which they could obtain a stable income. A descendant of the family had to pass another civil service examination by the third generation for them to maintain the gentry status. Educational success benefited the individual, family, and the lineage, and it became the primary avenue to success and fulfilling one's filial piety.

Relationship, not the individual, is considered to be a basic unit. The parent–child relationship provides the basis of the development of the self. Parental devotion, sacrifice, and support are important features of the traditional socialization practices that still remain in modern Korea (Park & Kim, 2004). A mother's job is to use her close relationship with her children to encourage them to expand their relationships and to succeed in life. She becomes a mediator between the home environment and the outside environment by socializing appropriate values and norms. As children grow up, they are expected to transfer their identification and loyalty from their mothers to their teachers.

The typical climate in Korean schools affirms the strong relational bond, pressures the student to strive for excellence, and encourages students to cooperate in a group. Children are taught to please the teacher and their attention is focused on the teacher. Even in a class size that is as large as 50, Korean students are attentive, devoted to doing their schoolwork, and motivated to do well. Finally, there is a high degree of agreement among adolescents, parents, and teachers about the value of academic achievement and how to attain it.

Empirical studies

An empirical study was conducted in 1997, prior to the economic crisis, to explore Koreans' perception of success and failure and factors that

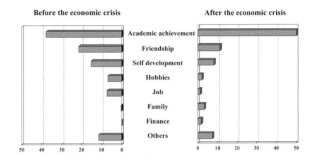

Figure 1. The most proud achievement.

contribute to the outcome. A follow-up study was conducted in 2001[1]. Using the indigenous psychology approach, an open-ended questionnaire was administered to a sample of Korean students. A total of 730 students in 1997 and 481 students in 2001 completed the survey. This paper provides the results of the following four questions:

1. Please list the achievement that you are most proud of and that is very important for you.
2. Please list the person who was helpful to you and specify your relationship to the person.
3. Specifically, what kind of support did they provide?
4. Overall, what do you consider to be the most important factor contributing to you success?

Figure 1 provides the results of the most proud achievement. The most frequent response was educational attainment, followed by friendship, self-development, and hobbies. Educational attainment became more important after the economic crisis. As for the person who provided the necessary support, parents (35%) were mentioned most frequently, followed by friends (27%), teachers (15%), and other family members (6%). In 2001, the role of parents (41%) and teachers (18%) increased, while the role of friends (14%) decreased. As for the type of social support received, emotional support (35%) was mentioned most frequently, followed by informational support (30%), providing a good environment (11%), and financial support (10%). A similar pattern was found in 2001: emotional support (39%), informational support (18%), and financial support (17%).

Figure 2 lists the factors that contributed to their success. Self-regulation (i.e., effort, hard work, and persistence) was mentioned most frequently, followed by good family environment, social support, personality, and positive thinking. In 2001, the importance of self-regulation, good family

---

[1] In 1998, the per capita GNP contracted by 32% and recovered to the 1997 level in 2001.

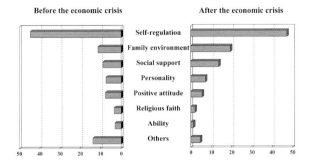

Before the economic crisis   After the economic crisis

Self-regulation
Family environment
Social support
Personality
Positive attitude
Religious faith
Ability
Others

Figure 2. The most important reason for success.

environment, and social support increased. A very small number of respondents reported ability (before = 3%, after = 1%).

When respondents were asked to list their most painful failure experiences, failure in academic achievement was mentioned most frequently (before = 45%, after = 46%), followed by human relationships (before = 23%, after = 18%), and self-regulation (before = 20%, after = 16%). As for the person who influenced the failure, most respondents blamed themselves (before = 51%, after = 67%), followed by friends (before = 26%, after = 18%), and parents (before = 8%, after = 8%). As for the most important reason for the failure, they reported a lack of self-regulation (before = 35%, after = 52%), followed by personality problems (before = 19%, after = 22%), and lack of ability (before = 9%, after = 8%).

Studies conducted with adults revealed a similar pattern of results (U. Kim & Park, 2003). Although men were most likely to list job success and women harmonious family, educational achievement came in second. They also viewed support from parents as being very important and self-regulation as the most important factor that contributed to their success.

In the follow-up studies, structured questionnaires were developed to examine the relationship between attribution style and academic achievement. Both students and adults were most likely to attribute their success to effort and their failure to a lack of effort and ability. Second, those students who attributed their success to effort had higher academic achievement (Park & Kim, 2004).

Finally, a 6-year longitudinal study has been conducted to examine the factors that influence academic achievement of Korean students. A total of 1012 Grade 6 students completed a structured questionnaire, 846 Grade 7 students, 796 Grade 9 students, and 656 Grade 11 students. The results of the path analysis indicate that parental factors (i.e., expectation, pressure, and social support) and

relational factors (i.e., respect for parents and a sense of indebtedness to parents) increased adolescents' self-efficacy, achievement motivation, and studying time, which in turn increased their academic achievement. In other words, close parent–child relationship and social support were important factors in elevating adolescents' self-efficacy, achievement motivation, and studying time, which in turn increased their academic achievement in subsequent years. Support from teachers and friends had an influence on adolescents' academic achievement when they were young, but this influence gradually waned with time.

DISCUSSION

Koreans view education as the most important life goal. People believe in effort, discipline, and persistence as the means to that goal. The sacrifice and support provided by parents are viewed as essential ingredients. Emotional support in the form of encouragement, praise, security, and understanding are valued. Koreans believe that ability can be acquired and personality can be polished through persistent effort and the support of significant others.

These results point to the limitation in Western theories. First, very few Korean respondents emphasize innate ability or personality. Instead they believe in self-regulation as being the most important factor that can lead to success or failure. Second, parental influence is very strong during childhood, adolescence, and even in adulthood. Third, close in-group members are highly influential, while professional relationships did not emerge as being important. Fourth, emotional support rather than informational support was reported as the more influential factor. Fifth, the self-serving bias has not been found in Korea. Finally, Western theories assume guilt to be negative and that it can lead to developmental pathologies. In Korea, it is considered appropriate that children feel guilty toward their parents for all the devotion, sacrifice, support, and affection they have received. Indebtedness is viewed as a positive interpersonal affect that promotes filial piety, academic achievement, and harmony.

The central difference between Western theories and the realities of East Asian societies have been summarized by U. Kim and Park (2004) and outlined in Appendix A. Results from international studies, such as PISA and TIMSS, point to limitations of existing Western theories in explaining the poor performance of American students and the superior performance of East Asian students. A series of empirical studies conducted in Korea verify the scientific values of indigenous psychology, which can more accurately explain and predict the educational achievement of Korean students.

REFERENCES

Bandura, A. (1997). *Self-efficacy: The exercise of control.* New York: Freeman.

Chorover, S. L. (1980). *From genesis to genocide: The meaning of human nature and the power of behavior control.* Cambridge, MA: MIT Press.

Kamin, L. J. (1974). *The science and politics of I.Q.* New York: Penguin Books.

Kim, H. C. (Ed.). (1992). *Asian Americans and the Supreme Court: A documentary history.* New York: Greenwood.

Kim, U. (2001). Culture, science and indigenous psychologies: An integrated analysis. In D. Matsumoto (Ed.), *Handbook of culture and psychology* (pp. 51–76). Oxford: Oxford University Press.

Kim, U., & Park, Y. S. (2003). An indigenous analysis of success attribution: Comparison of Korean students and adults. In K. S. Yang, K. K. Hwang, P. Pedersen, & I. Daibo (Eds.), *Progress in Asian social psychology: Conceptual and empirical contributions* (pp. 171–195). New York: Praeger.

Kim, U., & Park, Y. S. (2004). *Psychological analysis of human potential, creativity, and action: Indigenous, cultural, and comparative perspectives.* State of the art lecture provided at the International Congress of Psychology, Beijing, August 8–13.

Lynn, R., & Vanhanen, T. (2002). *IQ and the wealth of nations.* Westport, CT: Praeger.

National Center for Educational Statistics. (2000). *Mathematics and science in eighth grade: Findings from the Third International Mathematics and Science Study.* Washington, DC: U.S. Department of Education.

Nicholls, J. G., & Miller, A. T. (1984). Development and its discontents: The differentiation of the concept of ability. In J. G. Nicholls (Ed.), *Advances in motivation and achievement. Vol. 3, The development of achievement motivation* (pp. 185–218). Greenwich, CT: JAI.

Organization for Economic Co-operation and Development. (2003). *Education at a glance: OECD indicators.* Paris: OECD.

Park, Y. S., & Kim, U. (2004). *Adolescent culture and parent–child relationship in Korea: Indigenous psychological analysis* [in Korean]. Seoul: Kyoyook Kwahaksa.

APPENDIX A

Factors influencing academic achievement

Western theories	East Asian societies
High national spending	Moderate spending
Small class size	Medium class size
Biology	Culture
Disposition (IQ, personality)	Changeable, fluid
Primary control	Proxy and collective control
Cognition	Emotion
Active learning	Co-operative learning
Individualistic values	Parental expectation, pressure, and indebtedness
Personal motivation	Personal, relational, and social motivation
Ability attribution	Effort attribution

INTERNATIONAL JOURNAL OF PSYCHOLOGY, 2006, 41 (4), 293–297

Human ontogenesis: An indigenous African view on development and intelligence

A. Bame Nsamenang

Ecole Normale Superieure du Cameroun, Bambili Campus, Cameroun

Views on development and intelligence mirror mainstream Euro-American ethnocentrism and are presented as being applicable to all of human diversity. In contrast, an African worldview visualizes phases of human cyclical ontogenesis of systematic socialization of responsible intelligence in participatory curricula that assign stage-appropriate developmental tasks. In these curricula, knowledge is not separated into discrete disciplines, but all strands of it are interwoven into a common tapestry, which is learned by children at different developmental stages, who participate in the cultural and economic life of the family and society. This line of thought permits the integration of diverse ethnocultural realities and disparate theoretical threads into a common conceptual system—social ontogenesis. A theory of social ontogenesis addresses how, throughout ontogeny, children are co-participants in social and cultural life. The theory anchors human development as partly determined by the social ecology in which the development occurs and by how the human being learns and develops. Its seminal concept is sociogenesis, defined as individual development that is perceived and explained as a function of social, not biological, factors. But social ontogenetic thinking does not exclude nature; it assumes that biology underpins social ontogenesis. The biological commonality that the human species shares in the genetic code plays out into a bewildering diversity of specific individuality across ecocultures. Thus, contextualist theorists stress how different ontogenetic pathways and intelligences are situated in the socio-ecological contexts and cultural systems in which children are nurtured. The empirical grounding of this theory is based on impressionistic data from the Nso people of Cameroon, with supportive evidence in other parts of Africa. The universality of social ontogenesis offers an innovative impetus to conceptualize and generate developmental knowledge that empowers. It is a learning paradigm that permits the study of human development in the context of children's engagement of cognition when they are participants in cultural communities. This can expand visions and databases beyond restrictive Eurocentric grids.

Les points de vue sur le développement et l'intelligence reflètent l'ethnocentrisme euro-américain dominant et sont présentés comme étant applicables à toute la diversité humaine. En contrepartie, une vision du monde africaine se représente les phases de l'ontogenèse humaine cyclique de la socialisation systématique de l'intelligence responsable dans les programmes participatifs qui assignent des tâches appropriées aux stages de développement. Dans ces programmes, la connaissance n'est pas séparée en disciplines distinctes, mais tous ses enchaînements sont entrelacés dans une tapisserie commune. Cette dernière est apprise à des stages de développement différents par les enfants qui participent à la vie culturelle et économique de la famille et de la société. Cette ligne de pensée permet d'intégrer diverses réalités ethnoculturelles et des discours théoriques disparates dans un système conceptuel commun—l'ontogenèse sociale. Une théorie de l'ontogenèse sociale aborde la façon dont, à travers l'ontogénie, les enfants collaborent à la vie sociale et culturelle. La théorie s'enracine dans le développement humain comme étant partiellement déterminé par l'écologie sociale dans laquelle il apparaît et dans la façon dont l'être humain apprend et se développe. Son concept séminal fait référence à la sociogenèse, laquelle est définie comme le développement individuel qui est perçu et expliqué en fonction de facteurs sociaux et non biologiques. Mais la pensée ontogénétique sociale n'exclut pas la nature; elle suppose que la biologie sous-tend l'ontogenèse sociale. Les aspects biologiques communs partagés par l'espèce humaine dans le code génétique se manifestent dans une diversité déconcertante de l'individualité spécifique d'une culture à l'autre. Ainsi, les théoriciens contextualistes insistent sur la façon dont les trajectoires ontogénétiques différentes et les intelligences sont situées dans les contextes et les systèmes culturels dans lesquels les enfants sont éduqués. La base empirique de cette théorie est appuyée sur des données impressionnantes du peuple Nso du Cameroun, avec des appuis en provenance des autres parties d'Afrique. L'universalité de l'ontogenèse sociale

---

Correspondence should be addressed to Dr A. Bame Nsamenang, Ecole Normale Superieure, Bambili Campus, C/O P.O. Box 270, Bamenda, Cameroon.

---

http://www.psypress.com/ijp

DOI: 10.1080/00207590544000077

offre un élan innovateur pour conceptualiser et générer une connaissance du développement qui prend de la puissance. Il s'agit d'un paradigme d'apprentissage qui permet l'étude du développement humain dans le contexte dans lequel les enfants s'engagent à la cognition en tant que participants dans les communautés culturelles. Ceci peut étendre les visions et les bases de données au-delà des grilles restrictives eurocentriques.

*L*as perspectivas del desarrollo y de la inteligencia reflejan el etnocentrismo euro-estadounidense actual y resultan aplicables a toda la diversidad humana. En contraste, una visión del mundo africana visualiza fases de la ontogenia humana cíclica de la socialización sistemática de la inteligencia responsable en currícula participativos que asignan tareas apropiadas a los estadíos del desarrollo. En estos currícula el conocimiento no se separa en disciplinas discretas, sino que todas sus hebras se encuentran entretejidas en una misma tela, que los niños aprenden en las distintas etapas de su desarrollo, a la vez que participan en la vida cultural y económica de la familia y la sociedad. Esta línea de pensamiento permite la integración de diversas realidades etnoculturales e hilos teóricos dispares en un sistema conceptual común—la ontogenia social. Una teoría de la ontogenia social aborda como, a lo largo de la ontogenia, los niños coparticipan en la vida cultural y social. La teoría ancla al desarrollo humano como parcialmente determinado por la ecología social en la cual el desarrollo ocurre y como la persona aprende y se desarrolla. Su concepto seminal es la sociogénesis, definida como el desarrollo individual percibido y explicado como una función de factores sociales, y no biológicos. Pero el pensamiento de ontogenia social no excluye a la naturaleza; supone que la biología subyace a la ontogenia social. Los aspectos biológicos comunes que la especie humana comparte en el código genético se manifiesta en una diversidad desconcertante de individualidad específica de una cultura a otra. Por lo tanto, las teorías contextualistas subrayan cómo diversos senderos ontogénicos e inteligencias se sitúan en los contextos socio-ecológicos y en los sistemas sociales en los que los niños se crían. El fundamento empírico de esta teoría se basa en datos impresionistas del pueblo Nso de Camerún, con datos que apoyan de otras partes de África. La universalidad de la ontogenia social ofrece un ímpetu innovador para conceptuar y generar el conocimiento del desarrollo que proporciona poder. Es un paradigma de aprendizaje el que permite el estudio del desarrollo humano en el contexto en el que los niños se usan la cognición como participantes en comunidades culturales. Esto puede expandir las visiones y las bases de datos más allá de los enrejados restrictivos eurocéntricos.

INTRODUCTION

Indigenous psychologies connote indigenous roots. This notion involves a consideration of the process of immigration-emigration and human settlement in parts of the globe that are remote from ancestral or indigenous lands. Work on migration and settlement, however, suffers from bias, as it tends to be applied in reference to European emigration and settlement in other people's indigenous lands. Outside Europe and the US, the minority-majority status is not accorded a prominent place in social policy when it concerns the emigration and settlement of non-European peoples. Thus, the push to adopt the Eurocentric knowledge of mainstream psychology as "universal knowledge" has relegated knowledge of worldwide human development to a homogeneous, minority status. The heterogeneous and diverse knowledge about "the 85% plus of the world that is not part of Europe and North America" (Knutsson, cited in Pence, 1999, p. 15), has been marginalized as "indigenous psychologies."

This article presents a perspective on human development and intelligence that is indigenous to Africa south of the Sahara. Its framing principle is an African precept of not shredding human knowledge into discrete disciplines. In indigenous African education, all strands of knowledge are interwoven into a common tapestry (Moumouni, 1968), which is learned in a participatory curriculum. This line of thought permits the integration of diverse ethnocultural realities and disparate theoretical threads into a common conceptual system, that of social ontogenesis (Nsamenang, in press-b).

A theory of social ontogenesis addresses how, throughout ontogeny, humans engage social cognition as participants *in cultural communities* (Rogoff, 2003). Empirical support has been gleaned from impressionistic research with the Nso people of Cameroon (see Nsamenang, 1992, 2001, 2004; Nsamenang & Lamb, 1994, 1995) and substantiated by research in other parts of Africa (e.g., Asante, 1990; Babatunde, 1992; Beattie, 1980; Jahoda, 1982; Rogoff, 2003; Serpell, 1993; Zimba, 2002).

THEORETICAL MOORINGS AND CONCEPTUAL ISSUES

Social ontogenesis anchors human development partly within the ecology and social system in which the development occurs (Ngaujah, 2003). Stated differently, ecocultural factors are implicated in how the human person learns and develops (see Berry, 1994). In fact, contextualist psychologists have stressed how different ontogenetic pathways and intelligences are situated in the ecological and social systems in which children are nurtured. Thus, social ontogenesis is rooted in the traditions of ecological and cultural theorizing.

The seminal concept of social ontogeny is "sociogenesis," defined as individual development perceived and explained as a function of social, not biological, factors. Social ontogenetic thinking, thus, does not exclude nature, but assumes that biology undergirds social ontogenesis. In fact, the biological commonality the human species shares in the genetic code plays out into a bewildering diversity of specific individuality (Maquet, 1972) groomed in different ecocultural contexts. An Africentric view on development, therefore, focuses on nurture, to posit a theory of human development that gives much attention to the milieu in which development occurs (Ngaujah, 2003).

The plasticity of the biological timetable allows every culture to imprint its text onto processes of biological ontogenesis. It permits the transformation of a biotic system, the human being, into a cultural agent. Accordingly, it sounds plausible not to expect universally applicable milestones of human development, since every culture recognizes and assigns different developmental tasks to their perceived phases of human ontogenesis.

HUMAN ONTOGENESIS

Developmental science sometimes invokes notions of the human lifespan and life cycle, but does not articulate them. An African worldview envisions the human life cycle in three phases of selfhood (Nsamenang, 1992). There is a spiritual selfhood, which begins at conception, or perhaps earlier in an ancestral spirit that reincarnates. It ends with the ceremony to confer a name on a newborn. A social or experiential selfhood continues the cycle from the rite of incorporation or introduction of the child into the human community through naming, to end with biological death. Death is more acceptable in old age. An ancestral selfhood follows biological death.

In general, ancestors are the living dead (Mbiti, 1990), or spiritual presences in the affairs of the living. Some ancestors stand out as *the loving dead*. A cursory examination of the intentions and meanings of funeral rites and the memories people hold of loved ones for decades, even centuries, after their death can identify this class of ancestors to substantiate the universality of a selfhood that transcends the existential self. Some cultures claim the rebirth or reincarnation of their loving dead to complete the unbroken circle of being human (Zimba, 2002).

Social ontogenetic stages and developmental tasks

Social selfhood, the experiential phase of personhood, develops through seven stages. These include a period of the newborn, social priming, social apprenticing, social entrée, social internment, adulthood, and old age and death (see Nsamenang, 1992, pp. 144–148). Adding the two metaphysical phases of human selfhood to the seven stages of social ontogenesis completes the human life cycle.

Each stage of ontogenetic development is marked by distinctive developmental tasks, defined within the framework of cultural realities and developmental agenda (Nsamenang, 2000; Nsamenang & Lamb, 1995). We interpret development in African social thought "as the acquisition and growth of the physical, cognitive, social, and emotional competencies required to engage fully in family and society" (Nsamenang, 2005). For Rogoff (2003), this type of development is transformation in the individual brought about by participation in cultural activities. Such mentality primes Africans to guide child development as a process of gradual and systematic social integration. This conceptualization of human ontogenesis "differs in theoretical focus from the more individualistic accounts proposed by Freud, Erikson and Piaget" (Serpell, 1994, p. 18).

As children are initiated into and actively engage in cultural life, they gradually and systematically individuate into and assume particular levels of personhood, identity, and being. Individuation is the process by which the human being comes to a sense of self and personal identity in search of individuality—an imprint on the human person by the ecoculture. Within the African worldview, human beings not only need other humans but also social responsibility to individuate adequately and attain full personhood. Thus, a sense of self cannot be achieved without reference to the community of other humans in terms of being interconnected and enacting one's social roles. The social ontogenetic paradigm is premised not on an independent or autonomous frame; its foundational principle is an interdependent or relational script. It would be enriching to scrutinize the relational script as a challenge to, or alternative or complement to, the individualistic ideology of mainstream developmental psychology.

African parents expect children to assume social responsibility from an early age as a primary value over and above social cognition as an endstate (Nsamenang, 2005). As children grow, they are progressively assigned different roles on perception of their social maturity or competence. For African parents, social cognition translates into responsible intelligence, not in abstraction, but primarily as it enhances the attainment of social ends (Nsamenang, 2003b). The "concern with responsible ways of contributing to the social world" (Greenfield, Keller, Fulgni, & Maynard, 2003, p. 464) highlights responsible or social intelligence (Mundy-Castle, 1974; Nsamenang, 2003a). This value orientation infuses the socialization of responsibility into African parenting attitudes and programmes. In consequence, in African family traditions, "Socialization is not organized to train children for academic pursuits or to become individuals outside the ancestral culture. Rather, it is organized to teach social competence and shared responsibility within the family system and the ethnic community" (Nsamenang & Lamb, 1994, p. 137).

INDIGENOUS VIEWS ON COGNITION AND INTELLIGENCE

Indigenous developmental psychology can promote understanding of social cognition—how a given people learn and use knowledge. Jahoda and Lewis (1988) alerted the field to this possibility when they recommended moving "beyond the relatively narrow confines of cognitive development in cross-cultural studies" to "advance our understanding of the manner in which children come to adopt the prevailing social categories, values and norms in the context of their widening social relationships" (p. 29). The value of knowing not only how children grow up thinking, but also feeling and acting, in a given society cannot be overemphasized. As it targets developmental phenomena in context, social ontogeny permits understanding of theory in close proximity to actual psychological phenomena (Valsiner, 1997), hence its potential value in interventions.

The cultural content of intelligent behaviour

How children are taught or teach themselves to become competent members of their communities varies across cultures. In some societies children learn in schools; in others, they learn from active involvement in the life of families and communities. As African cultures recognize different phases of

children's emerging minds, they tacitly wed their participatory curricula to sequences of perceived cognitive capacities (Nsamenang, 2003b).

The embedded knowledge, skills, and values children learn from these curricula are not compartmentalized into this or that activity, knowledge, or skill domain, but are massed together as integral to social interaction, cultural life, economic activities, and daily routines (Nsamenang, in 2005). In principle, children are rarely instructed or prodded into what they learn, but discover it during participation. This depicts cognitive development as the unfolding of the abilities to generate the knowledge and skills with which to responsibly and increasingly engage with the world. Accordingly, the onus to understand the social cognition and intelligent behaviour of Africans lies in capturing shared routines and participatory learning, rather than in completing school-based instruments.

An evaluative criterion with which African parents determine intelligent behaviour is social responsibility (Mundy-Castle, 1974). To train responsibility, parents and caregivers allocate chores to children or send them on neighbourhood errands (Ogunaike & Houser, 2002). The "work" children do socializes cognition, values, and productive skills. It also generates knowledge and eases social integration. Some parents use evidence that a child has ability to give and receive social support, and notice and attend to the needs of others, as markers of mental and general developmental level (Weisner, 1987). In Zambia, for instance, adults "keep some mental tally of the proportion of errands that a given child performs adequately, and this serves as an index of how 'tumikila' the child is. In the short term, this attribute is used to choose which child to send on another such errand" (Serpell, 1993, p. 64). Episodes of a child's accurate enactment of roles feed into a history of that child's social competence; indeed, of their responsible intelligence.

In traditional Africa, the peer group plays a pivotal role in the development of this genre of cognition because, from toddlerhood, the child comes more under the purview of the peer culture than of the adult world.

CONCLUDING STATEMENT

It is unclear if developmental psychology that is ordained for universal applicability has matured beyond excluding "95% of the world's children" (Zukow, 1989, p. 2)! The Eurocentrism of the discipline pulls Africans "*away* from their roots, *away* from their own knowledge, and *away* from their own knowledge holders, into a chasm of dependency on others whose values and understandings have been shaped in very different cultures, histories and environments" (Knutsson, cited in Pence, 1999). Indigenous psychologies stand to enrich the discipline if developmental researchers could perceive their role first and always as a learner (Ngaujah, 2003). Accordingly, we have proposed a theory of social ontogeny as a learning posture (Agar, 1986) "to stir up interest and systematic exploration of distinctly indigenous patterns of development so that developmental research in Third World contexts may fertilize and expand the visions, methods, and knowledge of psychology beyond current (Western) moulds" (Nsamenang, 1992, p. 4).

REFERENCES

Agar, M. H. (1986). *Speaking of ethnography*. Newbury Park, CA: Sage.

Asante, M. K. (1990). *Kemet, Afrocentricity and knowledge*. Trenton, NJ: Africa World Press.

Babatunde, E. D. (1992). *A critical study of Bini and Yoruba value systems of Nigeria in change: Culture, religion and self*. Lewiston, NY: The Edwin Mellen Press.

Beattie, R. F. (1980). Representations of the self in traditional Africa. *Africa, 50*, 313–520.

Berry, J. W. (1994). An ecocultural perspective on human development. In E. Trickett (Ed.), *Human diversity*. San Francisco: Freeman.

Greenfield, P. M., Keller, H., Fulgni, A., & Maynard, A. (2003). Cultural pathways through universal development. *Annual Review of Psychology, 54*, 461–490.

Jahoda, G. (1982). *Psychology and anthropology*. London: Academic Press.

Jahoda, G., & Lewis, I. M. (1988). Child development in psychology and anthropology. In G. Jahoda & I. M. Lewis (Eds.), *Acquiring culture: Cross-cultural studies in child development* (pp. 1–34). London: Routledge.

Maquet, J. (1972). *Africanity*. New York: Oxford University Press.

Mbiti, J. S. (1990). *African religions and philosophy*. Oxford: Heinemann Educational.

Moumouni, A. (1968). *Education in Africa*. New York: Praeger.

Mundy-Castle, A. C. (1974). Social and technological intelligence in Western and non-Western cultures. *Universitas, 4*, 46–52.

Ngaujah, D. E. (Fall, 2003). *An eco-cultural and social paradigm for understanding human development: A (West African) context*. Graduate Seminar Paper (supervised by Dr Dennis H. Dirks), Biola University, CA.

Nsamenang, A. B. (1992). *Human development in cultural context: A Third World perspective*. Newbury Park, CA: Sage.

Nsamenang, A. B. (2000). Issues in indigenous approaches to developmental research. *ISSBD Newsletter, 1*, 1–4.

Nsamenang, A. B. (2001). Indigenous view on human development: A West African perspective. In N. J. Smelser & P. B. Baltes (Eds-in-Chief). *International Encyclopedia of the Social and Behavioral Sciences* (pp. 7297–7299). London: Elsevier.

Nsamenang, A. B. (2003a). Conceptualizing human development and education in sub-Saharan Africa at the interface of indigenous and exogenous influences. In T. S. Saraswathi (Ed.), *Cross-cultural perspectives in human development: Theory, research, and applications* (pp. 213–235). New Delhi: Sage.

Nsamenang, A. B. (2003b, February). *An African ontogeny of social selfhood: Social cognition or responsible intelligence?* Paper presented at the 2002/2003 Fellows Seminar Series, Center for Advanced Study in the Behavioral Sciences, Stanford University.

Nsamenang, A. B. (2004). *Cultures of human development and education: Challenge to growing up African*. New York: Nova.

Nsamenang, A. B. (2005). The intersection of traditional African education with school learning. In L. Swartz, C. de la Rey & N. Duncan (Eds.), *Psychology*. Oxford: Oxford University Press.

Nsamenang, A. B., & Lamb, M. E. (1994). Socialization of Nso children in the Bamenda grassfields of northwest Cameroon. In P. M. Greenfield & R. R. Cocking (Eds.), *Cross-cultural roots of minority child development* (pp. 133–146). Hillsdale, NJ: Lawrence Erlbaum Associates Inc.

Nsamenang, A. B., & Lamb, M. E. (1995). The force of beliefs: How the parental values of the Nso of Northwest Cameroon shape children's progress towards adult models. *Journal of Applied Developmental Psychology, 16*, 613–627.

Ogunaike, O. A., & Houser, R. F. Jr (2002). Yoruba toddler's engagement in errands and cognitive performance on the Yoruba Mental Subscale. *International Journal of Behavioral Development, 26*, 145–153.

Pence, A. R. (1999, April). *ECCD: Through the looking glass*. A keynote address presented at the ECCD World Forum, Honolulu, Hawaii.

Rogoff, B. (2003). *The cultural nature of human development*. New York: Oxford University Press.

Serpell, R. (1993). *The significance of schooling*. New York: Cambridge University Press.

Serpell, R. (1994). An African social selfhood: Review of A. Bame Nsamenang (1992): Human development in cultural context. *Cross-Cultural Psychology Bulletin, 28*, 17–21.

Valsiner, J. (1997). *Culture and development of children's action: A theory of human development*. New York: Wiley.

Weisner, T. S. (1987). Socialization for parenthood in sibling caretaking societies. In J. B. Lancaster, J. Altman, A. S. Rossi, & L. R. Sherrod (Eds.), *Parenting across the lifespan: Biosocial dimensions* (pp. 237–270). Hawthorne, NY: Aldine de Gruyter.

Zimba, R. F. (2002). Indigenous conceptions of childhood development and social realities in southern Africa. In H. Keller, Y. P. Poortinga, & A. Scholmerish (Eds.), *Between cultures and biology: Perspectives on ontogenetic development* (pp. 89–115). Cambridge: Cambridge University Press.

Zukow, P. G. (1989). *Sibling interactions across cultures: Theoretical and methodological issues*. New York: Springer-Verlag.

INTERNATIONAL JOURNAL OF PSYCHOLOGY, 2006, 41 (4), 298–303

Indigenized conceptual and empirical analyses of selected Chinese psychological characteristics

Kuo-Shu Yang

Fo Guang College of Humanities and Social Sciences, Ilan County, Taiwan

*A*n academic movement to switch from Westernized Chinese psychology to an indigenized Chinese psychology in Chinese societies (Taiwan, Hong Kong, and China) has existed for about three decades. Indigenous-oriented Chinese psychologists have conducted serious indigenized research on about 50 different broad topics. Kuo-Shu Yang's conceptual and empirical analyses on 3 of them are briefly reviewed in this article: (a) Chinese familism, familization and pan-familism; (b) Chinese psychological traditionality and modernity; and (c) theoretical and empirical analyses of the Chinese self. On the first topic, an indigenized conceptual scheme for the psychological components of Chinese familism at the cognitive, affective, and intentional levels was proposed. On the basis of the framework, standardized familism scales were constructed and used to study the relationships among the major components at each psychological level, using Taiwan students and adults as participants. In addition, the process of familization, an important aspect of Chinese familism, and its ability to form pan-familism in outside-family organizations, is briefly analysed. On the second topic, Yang empirically found that Chinese psychological traditionality (T) and modernity (M) were two independent psychological syndromes, each with five factor-analytically identifiable oblique components. Two separate standardized assessment tools were developed and applied in various empirical studies involving T and M. One study revealed that most T factors only negligibly correlated with most M factors, indicating a general trend for the two sets of components to coexist with each other during the process of societal modernization. Finally, on the third topic, Yang developed a four-part theory of the Chinese self from an indigenized perspective, based upon his conception of social vs individual orientation. The theory proposed that the Chinese self is composed of four self subsystems, viz., individual-, relationship-, familistic(group)-, and other-oriented selves, differing from each other in many respects. Yang and associates have conducted a series of empirical studies to examine a number of testable hypotheses derived from the theory. Findings from these studies are basically supportive.

*U*n mouvement académique faisant la transition d'une psychologie chinoise occidentalisée à une psychologie chinoise indigène dans les sociétés chinoises (Taïwan, Hong Kong et Chine) existe depuis environ trois décennies. Les psychologues chinois orientés vers la psychologie indigène ont mené des recherches sérieuses sur environ 50 grands thèmes différents. Les analyses conceptuelles et empiriques de Kuo-Shu Yang sur trois d'entre eux sont brièvement revus dans cet article: (a) le familisme chinois, la familisation et la panfamilisation; (b) la tradition et la modernité psychologiques chinoises et; (c) les analyses théoriques et empiriques du concept de soi chinois. Pour le premier thème, on retrouve une proposition de schème conceptuel indigène pour les composantes psychologiques du familisme chinois sur les plans cognitif, affectif et intentionnel. Des échelles standardisées de familisme furent construites sur la base de ce cadre de travail. Celles-ci furent utilisées pour étudier les relations entre les composantes majeures de chacun des plans, auprès d'étudiants et d'adultes taïwanais. De plus, le processus de familisation, un aspect important du familisme chinois, et son habileté à former le panfamilisme dans les organisations extérieures à la famille sont brièvement analysés. Pour le deuxième thème, Yang a empiriquement trouvé que la tradition et la modernité psychologiques chinoises étaient deux syndromes psychologiques indépendants, chacun comportant cinq composantes pouvant être identifiées par une analyse oblique. Deux outils d'évaluation standardisés séparés furent développés et appliqués dans diverses études empiriques impliquant la tradition et la modernité psychologiques chinoises. Une étude a révélé que la plupart des facteurs de tradition sont corrélés seulement de façon négligeable avec la plupart des facteurs de modernité, indiquant une tendance générale de coexistence des deux ensembles de composantes au cours du processus de modernisation sociétal. Finalement, en ce qui concerne le troisième thème, Yang a développé une théorie du

Correspondence should be addressed to Kuo-Shu Yang, Department of Psychology, Fo Guang College of Humanities and Social Sciences, 160 Linwei Rd, Jiaushi Shiang, Ilan Country, Taiwan 26247, ROC (E-mail: kuoshu@ntu.edu.tw).

http://www.psypress.com/ijp

DOI: 10.1080/00207590544000086

concept de soi chinois comprenant quatre parties, à partir d'une perspective indigène, basée sur sa conception de l'orientation sociale versus individuelle. La théorie proposait que le concept de soi chinois est composé de quatre sous-systèmes différant les uns des autres sur plusieurs aspects: le soi orienté vers l'individu, vers les relations, vers la famille (groupe) et vers autrui. Yang et ses collègues ont mené une série d'études empiriques pour tester un certain nombre d'hypothèses dérivées de la théorie. Les résultats de ces études appuient les hypothèses.

*D*esde hace aproximadamente tres décadas se observa una tendencia académica hacia una transición de una psicología china occidentalizada a una psicología china tradicional en las sociedades chinas (Taiwán, Hong Kong y China). Los psicólogos chinos con una orientación tradicional han llevado a cabo investigaciones tradicionales serias acerca de cincuenta tópicos generales. En este artículo se revisan los análisis conceptuales y empíricos de Kuo-Shu Yang acerca de tres de estos temas: (a) el familismo chino, la familización y la panfamilización; (b) la tradición y la modernidad en la psicología china y (c) los análisis teóricos y empíricos del concepto del yo en China. Respecto al primer tema, se propone un esquema conceptual tradicional para los componentes psicológicos del familismo chino a niveles cognitivo, afectivo e intencional. Se construyeron escalas estandarizadas de familismo basadas en este esquema, que se utilizaron para estudiar las relaciones entre los componentes principales de cada nivel psicológico, aplicándolas a estudiantes y adultos taiwaneses. Se analizan, además, el proceso de familización, elemento importante del familismo chino, y su capacidad para crear un panfamilismo en organizaciones de la familia externa. En el segundo tópico, Yang encontró empíricamente que la tradicionalidad (T) y modernidad (M) psicológicas en China eran dos síndromes psicológicos independientes, cada uno con cinco componentes oblicuos de análisis factorial. Se desarrollaron dos herramientas estandarizadas de evaluación por separado, y se aplicaron en varios estudios empíricos que involucraban a T y a M. Uno de los estudios reveló que la mayor parte de los factores T sólo se correlacionaban sólo de manera poco significativa con la mayor parte de los factores M, lo que indica que las dos series de componentes muestran una tendencia general a coexistir entre sí durante el proceso de la modernización social. Por último, en el tercer tópico Yang desarrolló una teoría en cuatro partes del yo chino a partir de una perspectiva tradicionalista, con base en su concepto de la orientación social contra la orientación individual. La teoría propuso que el yo chino está compuesto de cuatro subsistemas del yo, a saber, el yo individual, el yo de las relaciones, el yo familístico (del grupo) y los yos con otras orientaciones, todos los cuales difieren en muchos sentidos. Yang y sus colaboradores llevaron a cabo una serie de estudios empíricos para poner a prueba varias hipótesis verificables derivadas de la teoría. Los hallazgos de estos estudios son básicamente de apoyo.

Yang (2004b) recently made a systematic distinction between indigenous psychology, Westernized psychology, and indigenized psychology. He defined *indigenous psychology* as a discipline that applies the scientific method to the study of psychological and behavioural phenomena of people in a specific ethnic or cultural group, in such a way that the theories, concepts, methods, and tools used are highly compatible not only with the studied phenomena, but also with their ecological, economic, social, cultural, and historical contexts. Indigenous psychology is spontaneously, naturally, and gradually formed through an endogenous process without the intrusion and domination of a powerful alien scientific psychology. In contemporary world psychology, only psychologies in the Euro-American countries and the former Soviet Union are genuinely indigenous.

In the last two centuries, these Western indigenous psychologies have hegemonically dominated the initiation and development of scientific psychology in non-Western countries, which have thus generated almost the same kind of artificially transplanted psychology—that is, *Westernized psychology*. This kind of psychology, now prevalent in most non-Western societies, is formed by a process of academic Westernization through which non-Western psychologists uncritically adopt Western theories, concepts, methods, and tools in their research with local people as participants. Such a culture-ignoring psychology, or more aptly, imposed-etic (Berry, 1969) or pseudo-indigenous psychology, is nothing more than a distorted non-Western copy of Western indigenous psychology.

In recent years, increasing numbers of non-Western psychologists in an increasing number of non-Western societies have criticized the artificiality, superficiality, and incompatibility of their culturally alienated Westernized psychology in understanding, explaining, and predicting their people's mind and behaviour. They aim to transform their seriously undesirable psychology into an *indigenized psychology* through the process of quasi-indigenization. What they need to do is to consciously and purposely indigenize their research in such a way that the theories, concepts, methods, and tools created and used are sufficiently compatible with the studied local psychological and behavioural phenomena as structurally and functionally embedded in their ecological, economic, social, cultural and historical contexts.

The scientific psychology developed in major Chinese societies (Taiwan, Hong Kong, and China) is also a kind of Westernized psychology. But in the last three decades, an increasing number of Chinese psychologists, mainly those in Taiwan, have devoted themselves to the collective academic enterprise of systematically converting their Westernized Chinese psychology into an indigenized Chinese psychology that is able to understand, explain, and predict Chinese mind and behaviour much more efficiently (Yang, 1993, 1997a, 1997b, 1999). More and more indigenous-oriented Chinese psychologists have been endeavouring to conduct indigenized research on a wider variety of topics in various areas of psychology. There have been about 50 different topics on which serious indigenized studies have been completed. More than half of the topics fall into the field of personality and social psychology, followed by family and developmental psychology, clinical and counselling psychology, and organizational and managerial psychology, in that order.

Since the early 1970s, Yang and his associates have conducted indigenized research on such topics as familism and pan-familism, psychological traditionality and modernity, the Chinese self, Chinese basic personality dimensions, psychology of *yuan* (beliefs in predestined interpersonal affinity), relationship orientation, psychology of *ren* (forbearance and endurance), social-oriented achievement motivation, filial piety, and deviant adolescent behaviour. Empirical research on the first three topics will now be briefly reviewed.

CHINESE FAMILISM, FAMILIZATION, AND PAN-FAMILISM

Ever since ancient times, Chinese people have emphasized family as the centre of life, forming a strong sense of familism. At the micro level, Yeh and Yang (1997) defined familism as a person's complex system of social attitudes towards their family, family members, and family-related affairs, and conceived a familistic attitude as comprising three components, viz., cognitive, affective, and intentional (behavioural intention). They proposed a conceptual scheme for the major psychological contents of Chinese familism. According to the scheme, the cognitive contents of Chinese familism are the emphases on one's own family's prolongation, harmony, solidarity, wealth, and fame; the affective contents are the feelings of familial unity

(being one), belongingness, concern and love, glory, responsibility, and safety; and the intentional contents are the tendencies to engage in such behaviours as producing offspring, interdependence, forbearance, modesty, conformity, striving for family, respect for seniority, and in-group favouritism. On the basis of this framework, three standardized Chinese familism scales, respectively labelled the Familistic Cognition Scale, the Familistic Affection Scale, and the Familistic Intention Scale, were constructed to measure the three major aspects of Chinese familism.

Using these standardized scales, Yeh and Yang (1997) made further empirical analyses revealing that for both Chinese students and adults in Taiwan, the correlations among the three empirically identified cognition components (solidarity and harmony, family prolongation, and family prosperity) and among the three corresponding intention components (solidarity and harmony, family prolongation, and family prosperity) were all positive and substantial, and that the overall affect or feeling of familial unity was strongly positively correlated with all the cognition and intention components. These and other relevant results attest to the fact that the cognitive, affective, and intentional components of Chinese familism constitute a coherent psychological syndrome.

As Yang (1995, 1998) pointed out, Chinese people's family experiences are so deeply engraved in memory from childhood that they take their family as the prototype for the structuring and functioning of all the other organizations (including social, business, and even government ones). The structural and functional similarities between the family and outside-family organizations tend to make Chinese people transfer or generalize their familistic cognitions, affects, and intentions (and corresponding behaviours as well) to their life in other organizations. Through such a process, Chinese people familize other organizations to such an extent that they can think, feel, intend, and behave in them in a familial way. Yang (1993, 1998) labelled this complex process of stimulus generalization *familization*. The emergence and functioning of generalized familism in various kinds of nonfamilial organizations is called *pan-familism*. Yang (1998) reviewed research findings that revealed the existence of pan-familism in industrial and business organizations. An outstanding example of pan-familistic organizational phenomena is the Chinese paternalistic leadership style as recently defined, assessed, and studied by Farh and Cheng (2000).

CHINESE PSYCHOLOGICAL TRADITIONALITY AND MODERNITY

Yang's (2003) long-term programme of research on Chinese psychological traditionality (T) and modernity (M) may be divided into two stages. In the first stage (1972–1984), a measuring instrument, the Chinese Individual Traditionality-Modernity Scale, was constructed under the assumption that T and M constitute a unidimensional, bipolar psychological continuum. This scale was used in quite a number of empirical studies (for review, see Yang, 1996).

In the second stage, starting from 1985, Yang and his associates (Yang, 1996, 2003; Yang, Yu, & Yeh, 1991) adopted a new research strategy with two major assumptions: (1) T and M are two separate independent psychological syndromes, and (2) T and M are two multidimensional psychological syndromes. With these assumptions, and based on separate conceptual schemes of the contents of T and M, two assessment tools, the Multidimensional Scale of Chinese Individual Traditionality (MS-CIT) and the Multidimensional Scale of Chinese Individual Modernity (MS-CIM), were constructed with Chinese university students and adults as participants. The former scale measures five oblique T factors or components: Submission to Authority, Filial Piety and Ancestral Worship, Conservatism and Endurance, Fatalism and Defensiveness, and Male Dominance. The latter assesses five oblique M factors: Egalitarianism and Open-mindedness, Social Isolation and Self-reliance, Optimism and Assertiveness, Affective Hedonism, and Sex Equality (Yang, 1994, 1996, 2003; Yang et al., 1991).

Yang (1994) found that in all samples of students and adults, the total score of the five T components was only minimally negatively correlated with the total score of the five M components. This finding confirms the new assumption that Chinese T and M are two separate and distinct psychological syndromes. Further analyses revealed that the Male Dominance T factor substantially negatively correlated with the Sex Equality M factor, but the other four T factors only negligibly or minimally correlated with the other four M factors. This and other relevant findings were interpreted as indicating a trend for most T components to coexist with, rather than be replaced by, most M components with continued social change in Chinese societies. To explain this and other related phenomena, Yang (1988, 1994, 1996) proposed a cultural-ecological, interactionistic theory of psychological convergence and divergence during the process of societal modernization.

THEORETICAL AND EMPIRICAL ANALYSES OF THE CHINESE SELF

Yang (1995) termed the psychological pattern of strong autonomy and weak homonomy *individual orientation*, and that of weak autonomy and strong homonomy *social orientation*. He further proposed that Chinese social orientation consists of four (sub)orientations, namely, relationship orientation, authoritarian orientation, familistic (group) orientation, and other orientation. Individual orientation and the four social-oriented orientations respectively represent the five sets of characteristics of Chinese daily social interaction in five major life domains: (1) The domain of a person's interactions with himself or herself, (2) the domain of horizontal interpersonal interactions between two related persons with approximately equal power, (3) the domain of vertical dyadic interactions between two persons with unequal power, (4) the domain of a person's interactions with his or her own family or some other membership group, and (5) the domain of a person's interactions with unidentifiable nonspecific others, or the generalized other, as a real or imagined diffuse audience.

According to Yang (2004a), the five Chinese psychosocial orientations are regarded as the results of the Chinese self's successive differentiations between, and integrations within, each of the five life domains of daily social interaction in culturally specific ways in the Chinese lifeworld during the lifelong developmental process. The between-domain differentiations and within-domain integrations tend to make the psychological and behavioural functioning in each of the five life domains so functionally autonomized and structurally specialized that they form the five domain-specific subsystems, or more directly, subselves, that comprise the Chinese self. The five self subsystems are respectively named the individual-, relationship-, authoritarian-, familistic(group)-, and other-oriented selves. Since both the relationship- and authoritarian-oriented selves involve an interpersonal relationship, they are simply combined as the relationship-oriented self.

On the basis of Yang's (1995, 2004a) theoretical analysis of the Chinese self, a series of empirical studies has been conducted to explore the four domain-specific Chinese selves in terms of self-concept, self-esteem, and self-process. Since there are four Chinese selves, there should be four corresponding Chinese self-concepts (Yang, 1995, 2004a). Using university students from Taiwan and China as participants, Yang (2000) carried out a study to construct a tool for assessing the four domain-specific self-concepts. He began with a comprehensive pool of relevant items written on the basis of the conceptual scheme of the four Chinese selves and concluded with a factor analysis of the empirical data to identify the components of Chinese self-concept. Four major psychologically meaningful oblique factors were obtained, respectively labelled Individual-, Relationship-, Familistic-, and Other-oriented Selves. High loading items for the four factors were respectively chosen to construct the Multidimensional Self-Concept Scale for research with Chinese students and adults.

Also based on Yang's four-part model of the Chinese self, Weng, Yang, and Hsu (2004) attempted to develop an instrument for assessing four kinds of specific *trait* self-esteem as the major aspects of Chinese self-evaluation. Using university students from Taiwan and China as respondents, they obtained four major psychologically meaningful oblique factors, which were labelled Individual-, Relationship-, Familistic-, and Other-oriented Self-Esteem. High loading items for the four factors were respectively selected to construct the Multidimensional Self-Esteem Scale. In addition, Yang (2002) completed a study to analyse Taiwan students' components and changes of *state* self-esteem under success and failure situations, private and public conditions, and social- and individual-oriented life events. Yang's theory of the Chinese self has also been applied to the study of Chinese self-process, but the findings in this respect are beyond the coverage of this short article.

The reader may have noticed that Yang basically adopted a psychometric dispositional approach in the indigenous studies of all the three topics. This neither means that Yang has not relied on other approaches in doing research on other topics, nor that indigenous-oriented Chinese psychologists have all used the same approach. As a matter of fact, the methods employed by Chinese indigenous psychologists in their indigenized research are widely diversified, ranging from dialogics and heuristics, narrative analysis, analysis of stories and proverbs, and in-depth and semistructured interviews, to questionnaire surveys, standardized scales, and field and laboratory experimentation.

REFERENCES

Berry, J. W. (1969). On cross-cultural comparability. *International Journal of Psychology*, 4, 119–128.

Farh, J. L., & Cheng, B. S. (2000). A cultural analysis of paternalistic leadership in Chinese organizations. In J. T. Li, A. S. Tsui, & E. Weldon (Eds.), *Management and organizations in the Chinese context* (pp. 84–127). London: Macmillan.

Weng, J. Y., Yang, K. S., & Hsu, Y. (2004). Social- and individual-oriented self-esteem: Conceptual analysis and empirical assessment [in Chinese]. In *proceedings of the Conference on Chinese Self-process, Self-concept, and Self-evaluation*, held in Ilan County, Taiwan on February 28–29.

Yang, K. S. (1988). Will societal modernization eventually eliminate cross-cultural psychological differences? In M. H. Bond (Ed.), *The cross-cultural challenge to social psychology* (pp. 67–85). Beverly Hills, CA: Sage.

Yang, K. S. (1993). Why do we need to develop an indigenous Chinese psychology [in Chinese]? *Indigenous Psychological Research in Chinese Societies*, 1, 6–88.

Yang, K. S. (1994). Can traditional and modern values coexist [in Chinese]. In K. S. Yang (Ed.), *Chinese values: A social-science perspective* (pp. 65–120). Taipei, Taiwan: Kwei-kuan Book Co.

Yang, K. S. (1995). Chinese social orientation: An integrative analysis. In W. S. Tseng, T. Y. Lin, & Y. K. Yeh (Eds.), *Chinese societies and mental health*. Hong Kong: Oxford University Press.

Yang, K. S. (1996). The psychological transformation of the Chinese people as a result of societal modernization. In M. H. Bond (Ed.), *The handbook of Chinese psychology* (pp. 479–498). Hong Kong: Oxford University Press.

Yang, K. S. (1997a). Indigenizing Westernized Chinese psychology. In M. H. Bond (Ed.), *Working at the interface of cultures: Eighteen lives in social science*. London: Routledge.

Yang, K. S. (1997b). Indigenous compatibility in psychological research and its related problems [in Chinese]. *Indigenous Psychological Research in Chinese Societies*, 8, 75–120.

Yang, K. S. (1998). Familization, pan-familism, and organizational behavior [in Chinese]. In B. S. Cheng, K. L. Huang, & C. C. Kuo (Eds.), *Management in Taiwan and China, Vol. 4: Chinese legacies and management in Taiwan and China* (pp. 19–59).

Yang, K. S. (1999). Towards an indigenous Chinese psychology: A selected review of methodological, theoretical, and empirical accomplishments. *Chinese Journal of Psychology*, 41, 181–211.

Yang, K. S. (2000) *Social- and individual-oriented self-concepts: Conceptualization and measurement* [in Chinese]. Unpublished manuscript, Graduate Institute of Psychology, Fo Guan College of Humanities and Social Sciences.

Yang, K. S. (2002). *The components and changes of Chinese state self-esteem under success and failure situations, private and public conditions, and social- and individual-oriented life events: A scenario study.* [in Chinese]. Unpublished manuscript, Department of Psychology, Fu Jen Catholic University.

Yang, K. S. (2003). Methodological and theoretical issues on psychological traditionality and modernity research in an Asian society: In response to Kwang-Kuo Hwang and beyond. *Asian Journal of Social Psychology*, 6, 263–285.

Yang, K. S. (2004a). Towards a theory of the Chinese self: Conceptual analysis in terms of social orientation and individual orientation. In *Proceedings of the*

Conference on Chinese Self-process, Self-concept, and Self-evaluation, held in Ilan County, Taiwan on February 28–29.

Yang, K. S. (2004b). *Indigenous psychology, Westernized psychology, and indigenized psychology: A non-Western psychologist's view*. A keynote plenary address at the 17th International Congress of the International Association for Cross-Cultural Psychology held in Xi'an, China on August 2–6.

Yang, K. S., Yu, A. B., & Yeh, M. H. (1991). Chinese individual traditionality and modernity: Conceptualization and measurement [in Chinese]. In K. S. Yang & K. K. Hwang (Eds.), *The mind and behavior of Chinese people* (pp. 241–306). Taipei, Taiwan: Kwei-kuan Book Co.

Yeh, M. H., & Yang, K. S. (1997). Chinese familism: Conceptualization and assessment [in Chinese]. *Bulletin of the Institute of Ethnology, Academia Sinica, 83*, 169–225.

INTERNATIONAL JOURNAL OF PSYCHOLOGY, 2006, 41 (4), 304–319

Observers' decision moment in deception detection experiments: Its impact on judgment, accuracy, and confidence

Jaume Masip, Eugenio Garrido, and Carmen Herrero

University of Salamanca, Spain

Research into the nonverbal detection of deception has typically been conducted by asking observers to judge whether a number of videotaped statements are truthful or deceptive. In most cases, the behavioural segments used in this research have been very short. A typical result is that observers tend to judge the statements as truthful (truth bias). In the present experiment, observers watched a series of video clips showing senders answering three questions about an event that they had witnessed. Observers had to indicate whether each sender's statement was truthful or deceptive, their judgmental confidence, and when they had made their decision about the sender's credibility: during his or her first, second, or third answer. Competing predictions were made about the influence of the decision moment on the observers' judgments and accuracy. The results replicated most research findings reported in the US and North-European literature, including the truth bias phenomenon. However, the proportion of judgments of truthfulness decreased as observers decided later, particularly for the deceptive statements. This yielded an increase in accuracy in judging deceptive accounts. These results are consistent with the idea that initial credibility judgments are made heuristically, either because there is not enough information available or because observers are in the first, automatic stage of current attribution and person perception models. Heuristic decision making may produce a high proportion of judgments of truthfulness. Later judgments would be made in a systematic manner. The truth bias detected in deception research may be caused by researchers having used very brief and uninformative behavioural samples. The moment when observers made their decision had only a marginal negative influence on confidence.

La recherche sur la détection non verbale de la duperie a typiquement été conduite en demandant à des observateurs de juger dans quelle mesure un certain nombre d'affirmations filmées sont véridiques ou mensongères. Dans la plupart des cas, les segments comportementaux utilisés ont été très courts. Généralement, les résultats ont montré que les observateurs ont tendance à juger les affirmations comme étant véridiques (biais de vérité). Dans la présente expérimentation, les observateurs ont visionné une série de vidéos montrant des individus répondant à trois questions concernant un événement dont ils ont été témoins. Les observateurs devaient indiquer dans quelle mesure chaque affirmation des individus étaient véridique ou mensongère, leur niveau de confiance en leur jugement et à quel moment ils ont pris leur décision à propos de la crédibilité de l'individu: durant la première, la deuxième ou la troisième réponse. Des prédictions concurrentes ont été avancées concernant l'influence du moment de décision sur les jugements et l'exactitude des observateurs. Les résultats obtenus ont confirmé la plupart des résultats de recherche rapportés dans les écrits états-uniens et nord européens, incluant le phénomène du biais de vérité. Cependant, la proportion de jugements de véracité diminuait alors que le temps de prise de décision augmentait, ceci étant particulièrement le cas pour les affirmations mensongères. Ceci a mené à une augmentation de l'exactitude dans le jugement des mensonges. Ces résultats sont en accord avec l'idée que les jugements initiaux de crédibilité sont le produit d'heuristiques, soit parce qu'il n'y a pas suffisamment d'informations disponibles ou parce que les observateurs se trouvent dans un premier stage automatique d'attribution du moment et de modèles de perception de la personne. La prise de décision

Correspondence should be addressed to Jaume Masip, Department of Social Psychology and Anthropology, University of Salamanca, Facultad de Psicología, Avda. de la Merced, 109–131, 37005 Salamanca, Spain (E-mail: jmasip@usal.es).

The authors are grateful to the research assistants Gema Martín and Monica Sánchez, to Yago Reis and the actors Manolo Muñoz, Marta Calzada and José Romo, to the technician Javier Tamames, to José L. Vega, the Dean of the Faculty of Psychology of the University of Salamanca, for permitting us to use his office to record the tapes, and to two anonymous reviewers for their helpful comments on an earlier draft of the manuscript. This research was supported by the Junta de Castilla y León, Programa de Apoyo a Proyectos de Investigación, Ref. SA023/03.

DOI: 10.1080/00207590500343612

heuristique peut produire une proportion élevée de jugements de véracité. Les derniers jugements peuvent être faits de manière systématique. Le biais de vérité détecté dans la recherche sur la duperie peut être causé par les chercheurs qui ont utilisé de très brefs échantillons comportementaux contenant des informations limitées. Le moment auquel les observateurs prennent leur décision a eu une influence seulement marginalement négative sur la confiance des observateurs.

Normalmente, la investigación sobre la detección no-verbal del engaño se ha realizado pidiendo a unos observadores que juzguen si una serie de declaraciones en vídeo son verdaderas o falsas. En la mayoría de los casos, los segmentos conductuales empleados en esa investigación han sido muy cortos. Un resultado habitual es que los observadores tienden a juzgar las declaraciones como verdaderas (sesgo de veracidad). En el presente experimento, los observadores visualizaron una serie de fragmentos de vídeo en que aparecían unos emisores respondiendo a tres preguntas sobre un acontecimiento que habían presenciado. Los observadores tuvieron que indicar si la declaración de cada emisor era verdadera o falsa, su confianza en este juicio, y cuándo habían hecho su decisión sobre la credibilidad: durante su primera respuesta, la segunda, o la tercera. Se hicieron predicciones mutuamente excluyentes sobre la influencia del momento de decisión sobre los juicios y la precisión de los observadores. Los resultados replicaron la mayoría de los hallazgos de la investigación estadounidense y noreuropea, incluyendo el fenómeno del sesgo de veracidad. Sin embargo, la proporción de juicios de verdad decreció a medida que los observadores respondían más tarde, especialmente para las declaraciones falsas. Esto generó un aumento en la precisión obtenida al juzgar tales declaraciones. Estos resultados son consistentes con la idea de que los juicios de credibilidad iniciales se hacen heurísticamente, ya sea porque la información accesible es insuficiente o porque los observadores están en el primer paso, automático, de los modelos actuales de atribución y percepción de personas. La toma de decisiones heurística puede producir una alta proporción de juicios de verdad. Los juicios posteriores se harían de forma sistemática. El sesgo de veracidad detectado en la investigación del engaño puede deberse al empleo de muestras conductuales muy breves y poco informativas. El momento en que los observadores hicieron su decisión sólo tuvo una influencia marginal de signo negativo sobre la confianza.

The nonverbal detection of deceit has drawn the attention of many researchers over the last decades. In the typical deception-detection experiment, observers have to watch or listen to either recorded or live audio, visual, or audiovisual communications of a number of witnesses or suspects (the communication senders). After each communication, they have to indicate, normally in a form, whether the sender was lying or telling the truth (e.g., Miller & Stiff, 1993).

Using this procedure, researchers have studied the influence of a number of variables on observers' credibility judgments and their accuracy in detecting deceit (see Vrij, 2000, for an overview). However, a variable that, very surprisingly, has received little attention is the moment at which observers make their decision about the senders' veracity. Indeed, as time goes by, the communication sender provides progressively more information through his or her verbal and nonverbal behaviour.[1] Therefore, the later observers make their judgments, the more information they will have at their disposal on which to base those judgments.

This might have an impact on observers' judgments and accuracy. However, very often deception scholars have conducted their experiments using as stimuli videotapes that lasted only between 10 or 20 s (Feldman, Jenkins, & Popoola, 1979; Zuckerman, DeFrank, Hall, Larrace, & Rosenthal, 1979) and 60 s (Frank & Ekman, 1997). Although there are some cases in which the behavioural segments have been longer, only rarely have they lasted more than 120 s. Thus, not only have researchers neglected the influence of the moment at which observers make their decisions on their credibility judgments, but they have also used videotapes so brief that one may wonder whether they can contain enough information for observers to make a reasoned judgment. This might account for the finding that observers' overall accuracy in detecting truthful and deceptive performances is only slightly, and often nonsignificantly, above chance. Typically, accuracy falls within the 45–60% correct judgments, where 50% is chance accuracy (for reviews on observers' detection accuracy, see

---

[1] It could be argued that if the sender chooses not to communicate, then more time does not result in an increase in information. However, as Watzlawick, Beavin, and Jackson (1967) stated, it is not possible not to communicate, because even silence and stillness are informative. A sender trying not to convey information might, for instance, take a long time before answering questions, speak slowly, pause often, provide few descriptive details, and inhibit his or her body movements. Latency period, speech rate, number and length of pauses, quantity of details, and inhibitions of movements might be actual, perceived, or stereotypical deception cues (e.g., Vrij, 2000). Therefore, they are often very informative.

Bond & DePaulo, in press; DePaulo, Zuckerman, & Rosenthal, 1980; Kalbfleisch, 1985; Vrij, 2000). It is surprising that, among the many explanations that have been provided to account for this limited accuracy (see Kraut, 1980; O'Sullivan, 2003; Vrij, 2000), as far as the present authors know no-one has ever suggested that judgments may only be random, owing to the scarce information that can be contained in the brief behavioural samples used in deception research.

In the present report, a study is described that was designed to examine the influence of the observers' decision-making moment on their judgments, accuracy, and confidence. A number of senders were shown a videotape. Later on, they were interviewed about the facts depicted in the videotape. They had to answer three questions twice, once truthfully and once deceptively, while being videotaped. Each sender's answer to the first question was considered as Moment 1, the answer to the second question as Moment 2, and the answer to the third question as Moment 3. The observers watched each sender's performance on videotape. They had to write whether they thought the sender was lying or telling the truth, their confidence in that judgment, and when they had come to the conclusion about the sender's veracity—during the first, second, or third answer of the sender.

In addition to examining the effect of the decision-making moment on credibility judgments, accuracy, and confidence, we sought to replicate several typical findings of the deception literature. First, as we were interested in examining how the moment influenced some phenomena such as the truth bias, the veracity effect, and so on (see a description of these phenomena below), we had to examine in the first place whether these effects were apparent in this study. Second, we also tried to replicate the typical findings because most deception research has been conducted in the US and the UK, and cultural differences may advise against generalizing these findings to other sociocultural settings (see Bond, Omar, Mahmoud, & Bonser, 1990; Cody, Lee, & Chao, 1989; Ruby & Brigham, 1997; Vrij & Winkel, 1991).

The specific hypotheses tested are explained in the following sections.

ACCURACY, TRUTH BIAS, AND VERACITY EFFECT

As stated above, extant research has found that overall detection accuracy (i.e., accuracy in detect-ing both truthful and deceptive communications; see Miller & Stiff, 1993) falls within the 45–60% correct judgments range, either not significantly different from chance, or only slightly greater than chance. However, before asserting that, generally, accuracy in deception-detection experiments is poor, a distinction must be made between accuracy in detecting truthful statements and accuracy in detecting deceptive statements (see Masip, Garrido, & Herrero, 2004). Levine, Park, and McCornack (1999) observed that research demonstrates that people generally tend to lend credibility to the verbal and nonverbal messages conveyed by others; that is to say, they show a *truth bias* (see, e.g., the reviews by Bond & DePaulo, in press; DePaulo, Stone, & Lassiter, 1985; Kalbfleisch, 1985; Vrij, 2000; Zuckerman, DePaulo, & Rosenthal, 1981). Levine et al. also argued that this truth bias may give rise to a *veracity effect*, that is, accuracy in judging truthful statements will be significantly greater than accuracy in judging deceptive statements. In a series of three experiments, they repeatedly found that truth-detection accuracy was significantly greater than lie-detection accuracy (veracity effect). Also, accuracy in detecting the truthful statements was significantly greater than chance, while accuracy in detecting the deceptive statements was significantly lower than chance. This veracity effect was caused by a truth bias among observers. Indeed, the proportion of judgments of truthfulness was significantly greater than the actual distribution of truths and lies (truth bias), and a significant positive correlation was found between the proportion of judgments of truthfulness (hereafter PJT) and accuracy at detecting truthful statements, while a significant negative correlation was found between the PJT and accuracy at detecting deceptive statements. Levine et al. concluded that, since the overall accuracy rate blurs the differences between the detection of truthful and deceptive statements, deception researchers should report two separate accuracy measures, one for the truthful statements and one for the deceptive ones.

In view of the above arguments and findings of Levine et al. (1999), we posed the following hypotheses:

- *H1:* The observers will display a veracity effect:
    H1a: Accuracy in judging truthful statements will be significantly greater than accuracy in judging deceptive statements.
    H1b: Accuracy in judging truthful statements will be significantly greater than

chance, while accuracy in judging deceptive statements will be significantly lower than chance.

- *H2:* Observers will also show a truth bias: The frequency of judgments of truthfulness will be significantly greater than the frequency of judgments of deceptiveness.
- *H3:* This truth bias will account for the veracity effect. Thus, a significant positive correlation will be found between the PJT and accuracy in detecting truthful statements, and a significant negative correlation will be found between the PJT and accuracy in detecting deceptive statements.

The effects of the moment observers make their decision on the PJT and accuracy

Although these results should be expected generally, the moment observers make their decision might have an impact on the PJT and accuracy. There are at least two alternative ways this might happen, thus, two competing sets of predictions were made. First, from a systematic vs heuristic information processing framework, the PJT could be expected to decrease over time, particularly for the deceptive statements, while accuracy could be expected to increase over time.

These predictions are based on certain attribution and person perception theories, such as Fiske and Neuberg's (1990), Gilbert's (1989; Gilbert & Malone, 1995) or Trope's (1986). A common characteristic of these theoretical models is that they comprise several stages, the first of which is automatic, producing an immediate first impression based on a heuristic mode of processing. Only in a subsequent stage can the perceiver adjust his or her initial impressions. This requires a systematic way of processing information, which is effortful and requires cognitive resources (Chaiken, Liberman, & Eagly, 1989; Chen & Chaiken, 1999).

In the deception-detection domain, if credibility judgments are made very early (or if the behavioural segments to be judged are too brief), then observers are in the first, automatic step of these attribution and person-perception models. Also, observers may lack information to be processed in a systematic way in order to make a reasoned judgment, because the behavioural sample is so brief that it contains very little information. Therefore, the observers, requested by the experimenter to make a prompt credibility judgment, will make a heuristic judgment. And, normally,

heuristic credibility judgments are judgments of truthfulness. For example, Stiff, Kim, and Ramesh (1992) conceptualized the truth bias as a cognitive heuristic. Also, Millar and Millar (1997) found a more pronounced truth bias under conditions of low cognitive capacity than under conditions of high cognitive capacity. Finally, Gilbert, Krull, and Malone (1990) found that interrupting the participants' processing of information increased the likelihood of them considering false linguistic or iconic propositions to be true, but not the likelihood of them considering true propositions to be false. The authors concluded that merely comprehending a proposition increases the likelihood of initially representing it as true, even if the proposition is actually false. Only in a further stage are respondents able to critically assess its veracity. All these findings suggest that initial credibility judgments should be judgments of truthfulness.

However, as time goes by, the PJT should decrease. First, because observers will reach a later stage in their perception process, so that the automatic initial impression can be changed. Second, because the growing amount of information will allow observers to make a reasoned judgment. If, in addition, it is assumed that, when processing the senders' information in a systematic way, the observers are somewhat capable of discriminating between truthful and deceptive testimonies,[2] then the decrease in the PJT will be much more pronounced in judging deceptive statements than in judging truthful statements, since the correct identification of the latter would lead observers to make judgments of truthfulness.

These processes should have an impact on accuracy. If the PJT decreases over time, especially in judging the deceptive statements, then accuracy in judging the deceptive statements will increase. Also, if, when judging truthful accounts, the PJT decreases slightly, does not decrease, or even increases, then truth-detection accuracy will also

---

[2]This assumption might seem questionable, since extant research indicates that human observers' accuracy in judging the senders' credibility falls within the 45–60% range. However, as stated in the text, these conclusions are largely based on research using very brief behavioural samples, forcing observers to make their judgments heuristically and preventing them from using enough information to make a more accurate judgment. Even in the studies in which longer behavioural samples have been used, it is not clear whether the observers waited until the end of the senders' performance to make their judgment. The common assumption that observers' judgmental accuracy is poor may be an artifact based on how deception research has been conducted so far.

decrease slightly, will remain the same, or will increase.

Thus, we posed the following hypotheses:

- *H4a:* The PJT will decrease over time, particularly for the deceptive statements.
- *H5a:* Accuracy in judging deceptive statements will increase over time.

The alternative predictions were based on Masip, Garrido, and Herrero's (2003b) report. Masip et al. explicitly examined the effect of the moment at which observers made their decision about the sender's credibility on observers' accuracy in detecting truthful and deceptive accounts. They argued that, since the information conveyed by the sender when telling the truth is accurate, the more information given, the more correct the judgments. This would yield an increase in the PJT and, hence, an increase in accuracy in judging truthful statements. Conversely, the growing information conveyed by the sender while lying is misleading, since the sender manipulates this information in order to create an apparently truthful statement (information management), and tries to convey the impression of him- or herself being honest (image and behaviour management) (Buller & Burgoon, 1996, 1998; Greene, O'Hair, Cody, & Yen, 1985; Vrij, 2000; Zuckerman et al., 1981). This would also result in an increase in the PJT and a decrease in accuracy in judging deceptive statements.

In a series of two experiments, Masip et al. (2003b) found partial support for their predictions. However, in their studies, Masip et al. used only one sender. This seriously questions the generalizability of their findings. Another limitation of Masip et al.'s experiments was the subjective nature of how the observers distinguished between the diverse moments. Masip et al. asked their observers to indicate when they had come to the conclusion that the sender was lying or telling the truth, at the beginning of the statement (Moment 1), at the middle part of it (Moment 2), or at the final moment (Moment 3). However, there were no clear boundaries between the critical time periods. Thus, what for some observers was Moment 1 may have been Moment 2 for others, and what for some observers was Moment 2 may have been Moment 3 for others.

In any case, based on Masip et al.'s considerations and findings we posed the following alternative hypotheses:

- *H4b:* The PJT will increase over time, for both the truthful and the deceptive statements.

- *H5b:* Accuracy will increase over time for the truthful statements, but will decrease for the deceptive ones.

CONFIDENCE

Research into respondents' accuracy in detecting truthful and deceptive messages has repeatedly examined observers' confidence in their credibility judgments. A meta-analysis of this literature concluded that, typically, respondents: (a) are unaware of how well they are doing in judging the credibility of truthful and deceptive messages; (b) display significantly more confidence in judging truthful statements than deceptive statements; and (c) are more confident in their judgments of truthfulness than in their judgments of deceptiveness (DePaulo, Charlton, Cooper, Lindsay, & Muhlenbruck, 1997).

In line with these findings we predicted that:

- *H6:* Confidence in judging truthful accounts will be significantly higher than confidence in judging deceptive accounts.
- *H7:* Observers' confidence in their truthfulness judgments will be significantly greater than their confidence in their deceptiveness judgments.

The effects of the moment at which observers make their decision on observers' confidence

Few researchers have examined whether observers' confidence in their credibility judgments changes over time. Granhag and Strömwall (2001) conducted a study in which senders were interviewed three times about the same facts. One sample of observers had to judge the senders' credibility twice: first after watching the first interview, and then after watching the remaining two interviews. Granhag and Strömwall found that observers placed more confidence in their second judgment than in their first judgment. This might be due to the greater amount of information available to observers when they made the second judgment, or to them having a chance to test their initial hypotheses about the truthfulness of the first statement. However, unlike the observers in our study, Granhag and Strömwall's observers made two separate judgments about the same statements.

The prediction for the present study, in which observers have to make only one judgment per sender, is unclear. On the one hand, those who "are certain of it" from the very beginning might make their decision about the sender's credibility earlier, since they feel there is no reason to wait. Thus, high confidence scores may be expected at Moment 1. However, those who have doubts about the senders' veracity will wait until they are sure enough to make a judgment. They can feel confident at Moment 2 or at Moment 3, in which case they will make their judgments at these moments. In this case, confidence would not change over time. Also, it is possible that Moment 3 arrives, observers must make a judgment, and they are still uncertain about the senders' veracity. Therefore, they will score low in confidence. In this case, confidence would decrease over time. In view of these conflicting alternatives no specific hypothesis was posed about the influence of the moment of decision on observers' confidence, but the issue was examined.

In order to test the above hypotheses, a study was conducted. The study was similar to that of Masip et al. (2003b), but the weaknesses of their design were addressed. Thus, in the present experiment: (a) 24 senders (not just 1) lied and told the truth about the facts they had witnessed on a videotape; and (b) these senders were asked three questions so that each observer's answer to the first question could be considered as Moment 1, the answer to the second question as Moment 2, and the answer to the third question as Moment 3. Thus, clear and unambiguous "markers" were used to differentiate between the three time periods of interest.

METHOD

Stimuli collection

Participants

Twenty-four undergraduate students of criminology at a Spanish University (13 females and 11 males; mean age 20.89 years, age range 18–29 years) volunteered to participate as senders in the study.

Procedure

Creating the videotapes to be shown to the senders. In the present experiment, each sender watched a videotape in which three characters appeared. One of these characters committed an offence. After watching the videotape, the senders were asked three questions: One about each of the three characters in the tape. They had to lie and tell the truth in response to these questions while being videorecorded. The tapes containing the

senders' statements were later edited and shown to observers who had to judge whether each sender was lying or telling the truth. Each observer watched 12 three-answer statements. Six of such statements were truthful, while the remaining six were deceptive.

If all six truthful statements to be watched by any particular observer were based on the same facts, then the same statement would be repeated six times (i.e., six different senders would tell exactly the same story). As a result, towards the end of the 12-statement series, observers would know that those statements that were being repeated once and again (up to six times) were probably truthful. Therefore, instead of showing only one videotape to senders, we decided to show them two. This would decrease the number of repeated truthful statements to be watched by any particular observer from six to three. However, at the same time, certain characteristics of these tapes had to be kept constant so as not to influence the dependent measures. More specifically: (a) the characters had to be the same; (b) the offence and the general facts, as well as the physical setting, also had to be the same; and (c) each character had to perform different actions in each videotape.

Two scripts that met these conditions were written by the first author. The characters were a woman, a man with a moustache, and a man wearing a suit. The woman and the man with the moustache came into a waiting room. The second to come, who was carrying a briefcase and looked nervous, asked the other visitor the time. After a short while, the man wearing a suit came in and invited the first visitor to enter his office. The second one asked whether s/he could go in first, since s/he was in a hurry because s/he had to make a payment and the shops were about to close. S/he added, pointing to the briefcase, that s/he had just got the money from the bank. The man in the suit told them that they could go in together. Once inside his office, the man in the suit and the second visitor arranged something to do with a document. After that, the second visitor left, leaving his/her briefcase full of money on the office desk. Then, the first visitor, when the man in the suit was not looking, seized the briefcase and asked whether s/he could leave for a minute to check whether s/he had shut the door of his/her car.

The roles of the woman and the man with the moustache were exchanged in the two versions of the tape. Also, the actions performed by the man in a suit and the second visitor were different in each videotape. In addition, in one tape the man in a suit accompanied the second visitor to the door of his office to say goodbye, while in the other tape he said goodbye from behind his desk. Finally, in one tape the man wearing a suit gave permission to the first visitor to leave, while in the other tape he realized that the first visitor had taken the second visitor's briefcase and adopted a harsh attitude towards him.

Three semiprofessional actors played the role of the three characters. Their performances were videorecorded. The setting was the waiting room and the office of the Dean of the Faculty of Psychology of the authors' university. The videos were recorded on a Saturday evening, when the building was closed and no one would interrupt the recording session. Later on, a technician edited the videotapes. He was asked to use the same shots in both videotapes, since they had to be as similar as possible except for the critical differences. The final tapes lasted over 3 minutes.

Interviewing senders. Criminology students at the Faculty of Law were recruited to participate as senders in the experiment. In order to motivate them, the senders were challenged to lie convincingly. They were told that after observers had made their judgments, a list with their names ranked according to their lying ability would be posted on a board. They were encouraged to lie convincingly in order to appear at the top of the list.

Twenty-four students volunteered and signed informed consent forms. They were cited to go to the Faculty of Psychology one at a time. Each sender was received by a research assistant in the faculty hall and was escorted to a room where a second research assistant told him or her that s/he had to watch a videotape and that, after 10 minutes during which s/he could prepare his or her answers, s/he would be asked some questions about the facts depicted in the tape.

Then the videotape was shown to the sender. Afterwards, the second research assistant told him or her that she was going to bring him or her to another room where an interviewer would ask some questions about what each character in the videotape did. She told the sender that the interviewer would ask those questions twice. In one case s/he had to tell the truth, while in the other case s/he had to lie. The research assistant announced that she was leaving for 10 minutes, so that s/he (the sender) could prepare his or her statements. This was done because in actual situations, such as police interviews of witnesses, the interviewee is not questioned immediately, but after some time, and can anticipate the kind of questions that will be made and plan in advance the answers that s/he will provide.

She left the room, and after 10 minutes the first research assistant came in and accompanied the sender to another room. The first author, who acted as the interviewer, received the sender and asked him or her to sit down on a chair located in front of two videocameras, one of which recorded the sender's face while the other recorded his or her full body. Only the full-body recordings were used in the experiment described in the present report. The cameras were placed behind the interviewer's chair in such a way that the interviewer did not appear on the videotapes.

In order to create a rapport with the sender, as well as to allow him or her to relax—since the presence of the two videocameras was somewhat intimidating—the interviewer and the interviewee spoke for about 10 minutes about informal topics unrelated to the research while the cameras were already functioning. Then, the interviewer told the interviewee that he was going to ask three questions and that each question would deal with the actions of one of the three characters in the videotape. He also announced that he was going to ask the questions twice, and that the sender was expected to tell the truth (to lie in the alternative condition) the first time (first interview) and to lie (to tell the truth in the alternative condition) the second time the three questions were asked (second interview). At this point, in order to increase his or her motivation, the sender was reminded of the contest and the liars' ranking, and the need to make an effort to lie convincingly was stressed.

All the questions in the interview had the same structure: "Describe in detail what the man with a moustache (the man in a suit / the woman) did; I remind you that you have to tell the truth (lie)." The interviewer was blind with regard to the tape that that individual sender had watched. After both interviews were completed, the interviewer invited the sender to ask any questions about the procedure, answered those questions, debriefed the sender, and thanked him or her for participating.

A series of variables were counterbalanced. Thus, while one half of the senders watched the first version of the videotape, the other half watched the second version. In each case, the order of the three questions was also counterbalanced, so that each question was in the same location (1st, 2nd or 3rd place) within the question sequence the same number of times. Whether senders were first requested to lie and then to tell the truth or vice-versa was also counterbalanced. Finally, an effort was made to have a male and a female sender within each cell of the video version × question sequence × lying-truthtelling order matrix. The study design is summarized in Table 1.

TABLE 1
Study design and video composition (statements in each video and their order)

Version of senders' videotape	Sequence of questions[a]	Interview order[b]	Observers' tapes[c]				Statement order in observers' tapes
			A1	A2	B1	B2	
Version 1	1-2-3	T-D	1D	2T	1T	2D	2nd
		D-T	3T	4D	3D	4T	12th
	2-3-1	T-D	5D	6T	5T	6D	9th
		D-T	7T	8D	7D	8T	10th
	3-1-2	T-D	9D	10T	9T	10D	6th
		D-T	11T	12D	11D	12T	4th
Version 2	1-2-3	T-D	13D	14T	13T	14D	7th
		D-T	15T	16D	15D	16T	3rd
	2-3-1	T-D	17D	18T	17T	18D	8th
		D-T	19T	20D	19D	20T	5th
	3-1-2	T-D	21D	22T	21T	22D	1st
		D-T	23T	24D	23D	24T	11th

[a]1: "Describe in detail what the man with a moustache did"; 2: "Describe in detail what the woman did"; 3: "Describe in detail what the man in a suit did."

[b]D-T: deceptive-truthful, that is, the sender lied in the first interview and told the truth in the second interview; T-D: truthful-deceptive, that is, the sender told the truth in the first interview and lied in the second interview.

[c]A1, A2, B1, B2: see text; 1D: deceptive statement of Sender 1; 2T: truthful statement of Sender 2; etc.

For example, in the first row we can see that Senders 1 and 2 (statements 1D [sender 1's deceptive statement], 1T, 2D, 2T) had watched the first version of the videotape (Version 1), were asked the questions in the 1-2-3 sequence, and first told the truth and then lied (T-D).[3]

Video editing. The 48 statements that had been collected (a three-answer truthful and a three-answer deceptive statement from each sender; the interviewer's questions were removed) were edited to build four different 12-statement videotapes. The truth value of the statements, the version of the original videotapes, the order of the questions asked by the interviewer, and whether the senders had first lied and then told the truth or vice-versa, were counterbalanced in the tapes. In addition, the same sender never appeared in the same tape lying and telling the truth.

The resulting videotapes were labelled A1, A2, B1, and B2 (see Table 1). A random series of numbers ranging from 1 to 12 determined the order of the statements within each videotape. Thus, as shown in Table 1 (column on the right), the first statement contained in Videotape A1 was the deceptive account of sender 21 (21D), the second statement was the deceptive account of sender 1 (1D), and so on.

As stated above, each statement contained the truthful or deceptive answers to three questions. The questions had been removed from the videotapes that had to be shown to observers. On average, the senders' answer to the first question had a duration of 51 s and their answers to the second and third questions both had a duration of 52 s. In the stimulus videotapes, each series of three answers given by any particular sender was preceded by a 2-s dark screen with the heading "Subject X," where "X" was a number between 1 (the first sender in the tape) and 12 (the last sender in the tape). Within each statement, another 2-s dark screen separated the sender's different answers.

___

[3]It is apparent that the interviewer was not blind to the veracity of the senders' statements. This could potentially have influenced the way he interacted with each sender. While this is a frequent risk in much deception research, a number of safeguards were taken in this experiment to prevent this from happen. The interviewer was more an experimenter giving instructions to the sender than a real interviewer. In other words, the substantial part of the interview was not a free interaction, but was tightly scripted, and the wording of the questions was always the same. In no case did the interviewer interrupt the interviewee to make questions or comments. In addition, before the actual data collection began, the interviewer rehearsed his performance while interviewing mock participants in the same room where the actual interviews were to be conducted. Several research assistants were present in these rehearsals and provided feedback as to the verbal and nonverbal behaviour of the interviewer, which had to be neutral.

Data collection

Participants

The observers were 54 undergraduate students of psychology at a Spanish University (46 females and 8 males; mean age 22.41 years, age range 21–29 years). They received class credit for their participation.

Procedure

Observers were allocated to one of four separate groups. Each group had to judge a different videotape. Allocation of observers to the different groups was made randomly, except that the few male respondents were evenly distributed across groups. All respondents within a group were asked to attend the experimental session together. After they had entered a room equipped with a video and a TV monitor, an answer booklet was given to them. The instructions were printed on the front page of the booklet and the experimenter gave them orally as well. The observers were told that they were about to watch a series of 12 people making statements. Each person had watched a videotape and had been asked three questions about the events depicted in the videotape. They were informed that the questions had been suppressed from the tape. Also, they were told that the statement of each particular sender could be truthful or deceptive. It was stressed that it was not possible for a sender to be either telling the truth or lying in only one or two of his or her answers. Rather, either all three answers of any particular sender were truthful, or all three answers were deceptive. The observers were asked to determine whether each sender was lying or telling the truth. After they had watched the three answers of each sender, the experimenter would pause the tape in order for them to have time to express their judgments by ticking the "Lying" or "Telling the truth" box of this particular sender in the response booklet. Observers were also asked to indicate their confidence in each judgment on a scale ranging from 1 (*not at all confident*) to 7 (*absolutely confident*). Also, they had to indicate, for each judgment, whether they had made their decision concerning that sender's veracity during his or her first, second, or third answer.

Also, since there were still three truthful statements on each tape that were based on the same version of the videotape shown to the senders, it was important to prevent the observers from making cross-statement comparisons, because this could artificially increase their later judgments. Therefore, they were told that: (a) not all senders had watched the same tapes; (b) on most occasions, but not always, the videotapes that the senders had watched were very similar; and (c) on most occasions, but not always, deceivers did not drastically alter the facts depicted in the videotape they had watched, but introduced minor changes. Thus, as a result, truthful and deceptive statements were generally very similar. The observers were then advised to judge each statement independently from the others.[4] Also, the observers were told that there were three characters in all the videotapes watched by the senders: a woman and two men. They were also informed about the questions that the senders had been asked.[5]

After the observers had been given and had understood all these instructions, the experimental session began. The experimenter, placed behind the observers, used the remote control to pause the videotape after each statement, and did not press the "play" button again until all the participants had answered all the questions in the response booklet about this particular statement. After the observers had completed the task for all 12 statements, the experimenter thanked them for their participation, answered their questions, asked them not to talk about the study to those participants who had to act as observers later on,

---

[4]In order to examine whether accuracy for later judgments increased, manipulation check analyses were conducted. There were two sets of senders: odd senders and even senders. Odd senders were in videos A1 and B1, whereas even senders were in videos A2 and B2. The order of senders in A1 was the same as in B1, but those senders who lied in A1 told the truth in B1, and vice-versa (Table 1). The same can be said of A2 and B2. All videotapes contained 12 statements. Accuracy in judging the last 6 statements (which contained 3 truths and 3 lies) was compared with accuracy in judging the first 6 statements (also 3 truths and 3 lies) for both odd and even senders. These comparisons were not significant, $t(26) = 1.40$, $p = .173$, for odd senders, and $t(26) = 1.68$, $p = .104$ for even senders.

[5]The experimental instructions were tested on three samples. The convenience of including all this additional information was assessed. It became apparent from the comments of the participants in the pilot tests (undergraduate students who received the instructions and performed part of the task) that, unless they received this information, they assumed that all senders had watched the same videotape and then tended to compare different statements in order to assess their veracity. Furthermore, it was certain that, except for a few cases, the observers did not make major changes when lying. Also, since the questions had been removed from the tapes, we thought that telling observers what the questions were about would help them to focus upon the experimental task—instead of, for instance, trying to guess the interviewer's question. The pilot test supported our views. Observers in the actual experimental task were also informed that the three questions had been counterbalanced.

and informed them that they would be invited to attend a lecture where they would be debriefed.

RESULTS

Accuracy and proportion of judgments of truthfulness (PJT)

Accuracy

Overall accuracy (proportion of correct judgments) was very moderate (.54) but significantly greater than chance probability (.50), $t(51) = 2.50$, $p = .016$. As predicted in Hypothesis 1, accuracy in judging truthful accounts (.59) was significantly greater than chance, $t(51) = 3.04$, $p = .004$. However, contrary to our prediction, observers' accuracy in judging deceptive statements (.50) did not differ from chance, $t(51) = -0.12$, $p = .907$.

These results suggest that accuracy was greater when judging truthful statements than when judging deceptive statements. To examine whether the difference was significant, an analysis of variance (ANOVA) was conducted on the proportion of correct judgments. The independent variables were the value of truth of the statements (truthful vs. deceptive statement) and the stimulus videotape (A1/A2/B1/B2), with repeated measures in the first variable. A significant main effect for value of truth revealed that accuracy in judging truthful accounts was significantly greater than accuracy in judging deceptive accounts, $F(1, 50) = 4.80$, $p = .033$. However, as shown in Figure 1, this main effect was qualified by a significant Value of Truth × Videotape interaction, $F(3, 50) = 4.27$, $p = .009$. This interaction indicated that the strength of the veracity effect was not the same across all four videotapes—in fact, a nonsignificant trend, $t(12) = -0.92$, $p = .376$, in the opposite direction was found for B2. The main effect for the videotape was not significant in this ANOVA, $F(3, 50) < 1$.

The correlation between accuracy in judging truthful statements and accuracy in judging deceptive statements was negative and did not reach statistical significance, $r = -.23$, $p = .092$. As might be expected, both accuracy in judging truthful statements and accuracy in judging deceptive statements correlated significantly with overall accuracy, respectively, $r = .68$ and $r = .56$, both $ps < .001$.

Proportion of judgments of truthfulness

In support of Hypothesis 2, more judgments of truthfulness were made than judgments of deceptiveness: Across truthful and deceptive statements

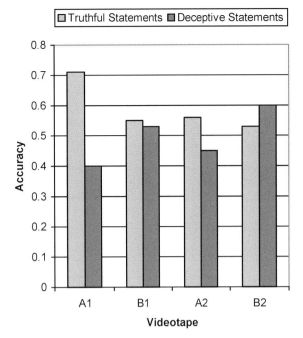

Figure 1. Accuracy rates.

the proportion of judgments of truthfulness (.55) was significantly greater than chance, $t(51) = 2.12$, $p = .039$. The PJT in judging truthful statements (.59) was also greater than chance, $t(51) = 3.04$, $p = .004$, but, in judging the deceptive statements, the PJT (.50) did not differ from chance probability, $t(51) = 0.12$, $p = .907$.

These results suggest that the PJT was greater when judging the truthful statements than when judging deceptive ones. An ANOVA was conducted on the PJT. The independent variables were the value of truth of the statements (truthful vs. deceptive statement) and the stimulus videotape (A1/A2/B1/B2), with repeated measures in the first variable. A significant main effect for the value of truth on the PJT indicated that significantly more judgments of truthfulness were made when the statements were actually truthful (.59) than when they were deceptive (.50), $F(1, 50) = 6.19$, $p = .016$ (Figure 2). This suggests that observers were somewhat capable of discerning between truthful and deceptive accounts, as already indicated by the accuracy results reported above (overall accuracy was greater than chance). The main effect for the videotape was also significant, $F(1, 50) = 4.27$, $p = .009$. In general, the statements contained in some videotapes were more often considered truthful than those contained in other videotapes (see Figure 2). Indeed, this effect is consistent with the above finding of a significant Truth Value × Videotape interaction on accuracy: The greater the PJT, the greater the proportion of accurate judgments in judging

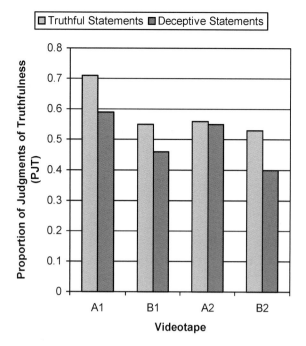

Figure 2. Proportion of judgments of truthfulness (PJT)

truthful statements and the smaller the proportion of accurate judgments in judging deceptive statements. Greater veracity effects were caused by greater PJTs.

Interestingly, the Value of Truth × Videotape interaction was far from significance, $F(3, 50) < 1$. This indicates that, despite the differences among the videotapes in terms of the veracity effect, the above main effect for the value of truth on the PJT was consistent across all the videotapes that were shown to observers.

As predicted in Hypothesis 3, the PJT across truthful and deceptive statements bore a significant positive correlation with accuracy in judging truthful statements, $r = .81$, $p < .001$, and a significant negative correlation with accuracy in judging deceptive statements, $r = -.76$, $p < .001$. As might be expected, the correlation between the PJT and overall accuracy was not significant, $r = .12$, $p = .395$. The correlation between the PJT in judging truthful statements and the PJT in judging deceptive statements did not reach statistical significance, $r = .23$, $p = .092$. Both the PJT in judging truthful statements and the PJT in judging deceptive statements correlated significantly with the overall PJT, respectively, $r = .81$ and $r = .76$, both $ps < .001$.

The influence of the moment at which observers made their decision

Since many participants, either in judging the truthful statements or in judging the deceptive

ones, did not choose to make any decision at Moment 1, at Moment 2, or at Moment 3, the moment variable could not be entered as an independent variable in the above ANOVAs. Instead, its effect on accuracy, the PJT, and confidence, was examined using correlations. Moment-1 judgments were coded as 1, Moment-2 judgments as 2, and Moment-3 judgments as 3. Then, these values were summed across truthful statements, across deceptive statements, and across both truthful and deceptive statements. Positive correlations between these variables and accuracy, the PJT, and confidence, would reflect increases in accuracy, PJT, and confidence as observers made their decisions later. Negative correlations would reflect decreases in accuracy, PJT and confidence.[6]

Accuracy. Overall accuracy did not change significantly over time, $r = -.01$, $p = .933$. For truthful statements, the moment–accuracy correlation was negative but nonsignificant, $r = -.14$, $p = .309$. For deceptive statements, this correlation was positive and marginally significant, $r = .24$, $p = .077$, revealing a trend for observers to make more accurate judgments of the deceptive statements the later they made their decisions.

Proportion of judgments of truthfulness (PJT). A statistically significant moment–PJT correlation indicated that the PJT decreased when observers made their decisions later, $r = -.29$, $p = .037$. While this reduction was very meagre for the truthful statements, $r = -.14$, $p = .309$, it reached a marginal significance for the deceptive ones, $r = -.24$, $p = .077$.

Moment in judging truthful and deceptive statements. The correlation of the moment variable for truthful statements with the moment variable for deceptive statements was positive and significant, $r = .34$, $p = .013$. This indicated that, regardless of the truth value of the statements, some observers consistently made their decisions earlier than others. As might be expected, the moment variable, when collapsed across both truthful and deceptive statements, was significantly correlated

---

[6]In order to conduct Pearson correlations the distributions must be normal. The skewness and kurtosis of accuracy, the PJT, confidence, and the moment variable (for truthful statements, deceptive statements, and across all statements) were calculated using the SPSS "frequencies" command and were then divided by their standard error. Most of the resulting values were lower than 1, and all of them were lower than 2. Therefore, the distributions did not depart significantly from normality.

with the moment variable for truthful statements, $r = .79$, $p < .001$, and deceptive statements, $r = .84$, $p < .001$.

Confidence

Descriptive results. Confidence across both truthful and deceptive statements was 4.18 on a 1–7 scale. Rates were 4.22 for the truthful statements and 4.15 for the deceptive statements. An ANOVA similar to those conducted on accuracy and the PJT was run taking the observers' judgmental confidence as the dependent measure. Contrary to Hypothesis 6, the truth value of the statements had no significant effect on confidence, $F(1, 50) < 1$. Similarly, neither the stimulus videotape, $F(3, 50) < 1$, nor its interaction with the value of truth of the statements, $F(3, 50) = 2.04$, $p = .121$, had any significant effect on confidence.

Confidence–accuracy correlations. In line with the results of DePaulo et al. (1997), the relationship between confidence and accuracy was not significant, $r = .13$, $p = .347$. When examining this relationship separately for truthful and deceptive statements, it was apparent that confidence and accuracy in judging deceptive statements were unrelated, $r = -.20$, $p = .156$. However, a significant correlation emerged between confidence and accuracy in judging truthful statements, $r = .32$, $p = .019$.

The influence of the moment at which observers made their decision. The correlation between the moment at which observers made their decision and their confidence in that decision was negative and marginally significant, $r = -.25$, $p = .066$. This effect was negligible for the truthful statements, $r = -.15$, $p = .280$, but was significant for the deceptive ones, $r = -.33$, $p = .015$. The later observers made their decision, the less confidence they had in that decision.

PJT–confidence correlations. Both the above significant correlation between confidence and accuracy in judging truthful accounts and the decrease in confidence over time when judging deceptive accounts could be accounted for by the relation predicted in Hypothesis 7: Greater confidence in judgments of truthfulness than in judgments of deceptiveness. First, if confidence in making judgments of truthfulness is particularly strong, the more judgments of truthfulness observers make, the greater their mean confidence

scores. If the statements are truthful, accuracy will rise as well. This would account for the above significant correlation between confidence and accuracy for the truthful statements. In support of this explanation, the PJT–confidence correlation was positive and significant for the truthful statements, $r = .32$, $p = .019$. Second, when judging the deceptive statements, when observers make their decision later not only their confidence decreases, but also the PJT. If greater confidence is placed in the judgments of truthfulness than in those of deceptiveness, then as the PJT decreases over time, so will the observers' confidence. However, for the deceptive statements, the PJT–confidence correlation was not significant, $r = .20$, $p = .156$. Finally, across both truthful and deceptive statements, the PJT–confidence correlation did not reach statistical significance, $r = .23$, $p = .092$.

Confidence in judging truthful and deceptive statements. Those observers who were more confident in judging truthful statements were also more confident in judging deceptive statements, $r = .74$, $p < .001$. This, coupled with the above findings that observers' confidence was unaffected by the statement truth-value, the stimulus videotape, or their interaction, suggests that some observers were more confident than others. As might be expected, overall confidence across truthful and deceptive statements was significantly related to both confidence in judging truthful statements, $r = .94$, $p < .001$, and confidence in judging deceptive statements, $r = .93$, $p < .001$.

DISCUSSION

Accuracy, truth bias, and veracity effect

Deception research has normally been conducted using very brief behavioural segments, and has led researchers to conclude that observers making credibility judgments show a strong truth bias. In this experiment, we examined how the length of the behavioural segments influenced the judgments, accuracy, and confidence of the observers. Also, we sought to replicate several typical findings of the US and North-European deception literature in a South-European country. The results indicate that, in line with the findings of extant research conducted in other countries (Bond & DePaulo, in press; DePaulo et al., 1985; Vrij, 2000), overall detection accuracy is poor but significantly greater than chance. However, when the truth value of statements was taken into consideration, following Levine et al.'s (1999) recommendations, a more complex picture emerged. Thus, as predicted in Hypothesis 1a, accuracy in judging truthful statements was significantly greater than accuracy in judging deceptive statements. Therefore, a veracity effect was apparent. Furthermore, although accuracy in judging deceptive statements was not below chance, accuracy in judging truthful statements was significantly greater than chance (Hypothesis 1b). This veracity effect seemed to be caused by a truth bias. Indeed, supporting Hypothesis 2, the PJT was greater than chance—or, in other words, significantly more judgments of truthfulness were made than judgments of deceptiveness. In addition, the PJT bore a significant positive correlation with accuracy in judging truthful statements and a significant negative correlation with accuracy in judging deceptive statements (Hypothesis 3). Also, the correlation between the PJT in judging truthful and deceptive statements was not significant. These results are generally consistent with Levine et al.'s (1999) arguments, suggesting that overall accuracy rates are misleading, since large differences, caused by the truth bias and veracity effect phenomena, are apparent between accuracy in judging truthful and deceptive communications.

However, some further considerations are pertinent. First, as stated above, the PJT across both truthful and deceptive accounts was significantly greater than chance. However, consistent with an accuracy rate above chance, the PJT was significantly greater when judging the truthful statements than when judging the deceptive ones. In fact, while in the former case it was greater than chance, in the latter case it did not differ significantly from chance. These findings question the notion that the increased PJT was merely due to a truth "bias." Although when judging the deceptive statements the PJT was indeed excessive (it should have been significantly lower than chance), the overall PJT across truthful and deceptive statements was greater than chance because of the contribution of the PJT in judging truthful accounts. However, if observers are assumed to possess some detection skills, their PJT in judging truthful statements *must* be greater than chance, as well as greater than their PJT in judging deceptive statements. But this is not indicative of a truth bias, but rather of observers' accuracy in detecting truthful statements.[7]

Second, the moment when observers made their decisions correlated significantly with the PJT. As expected if initial credibility judgments are automatic while later judgments are made on the basis of a systematic processing of information, the PJT decreased over time. Furthermore, it decreased more for the deceptive statements than for the truthful ones—for which the reduction did not even approach significance. This reflects an increased ability among observers to progressively discriminate between truthful and deceptive accounts, as would be expected if they progressively engaged in systematic information processing. The nonreduction in the PJT in judging truthful statements does not reflect the existence of a truth "bias," since the accurate judgments of the truthful statements are indeed judgments of truthfulness. These results support Hypothesis 4a, and are contrary to Hypothesis 4b.

The changes in the PJT had an impact on accuracy. Since the PJT in judging truthful statements did not change over time, accuracy in these statements was similar at all three moments. Also, since the PJT in judging deceptive accounts decreased over time, accuracy in judging deceptive statements increased. However, the progressive differentiation between truthful and deceptive statements over time was not sufficient to increase overall detection accuracy (i.e., accuracy in detecting both truthful and deceptive accounts).

These results do not support Masip et al.'s (2003b) hypotheses predicting an increase in accuracy in judging the truthful accounts and a decrease in judging the deceptive ones. Instead, they point to the heuristic vs systematic information processing explanation. Previous research conducted by Granhag and Strömwall (2000, 2001) points in the same direction. They found a significant increase in accuracy when the same observers made two credibility judgments of the same senders. The increase was marginal for the deceptive statements and significant for the truthful ones. Although it was not a central point of their study and therefore they overlooked it, it is interesting that Granhag and Strömwall's results further support our heuristic vs systematic processing prediction: in their study, not only did the PJT

---

[7]An exaggerated number of judgments of truthfulness were only apparent when deceptive accounts were judged. Although the PJT when judging the truthful accounts (.59) was greater than chance, it was far from 1. As for the deceptive statements, the .50 PJT might reflect, as an anonymous reviewer suggested, that participants relied on mere guesswork. Alternatively, since the moment–PJT correlation was significant, it can be assumed that at Moment 1 the PJT in judging deceptive statements was greater than the average .50 rate, whereas at Moment 3 it was lower. Therefore, a truth bias was presumably present when judgments of deceptive statements were made early. Unfortunately, the design of this study made it difficult to calculate the PJT separately at Moments 1, 2, and 3. Ongoing research is addressing this issue.

decrease for the deceptive statements (although only marginally), but it also increased significantly for the truthful ones, thus reflecting an increased ability to distinguish between both kinds of statements. However, Granhag and Strömwall's results are not fully comparable with the present findings. For example, their temporal variable was a within-subject one, while our participants made just one judgment per sender. This might have influenced the results. Furthermore, Granhag and Strömwall explored the effects on accuracy of the *number of interviews* watched by observers, whereas we explored, *within the same interview*, the impact that the moment the decision about the senders' veracity was made had on the PJT and accuracy. Indeed, Granhag and Strömwall's second and third interviews did not consist of participants' answers to just one question, while our Moments 2 and 3 consisted of answers to single questions. Thus, presumably, Granhag and Strömwall's second and third interviews were longer and more informative than our participants' answers to the second and third questions. In addition, while Granhag and Strömwall's first interview was made 3 hours after having watched a staged event, the second interview 4 days later, and the last interview 1 week later, our first question was made a few minutes after the sender had watched the videotape, and the second and third questions were made immediately after that. Changes in memory over time, rehearsal time, and similar, are variables that might influence the senders' statement and the observers' judgments and accuracy. Despite these and other differences, the results of both studies are consistent with the heuristic vs systematic processing hypotheses. This strongly supports the validity of these hypotheses.

Confidence

In line with the results of DePaulo et al.'s (1997) meta-analysis, the correlation between confidence and accuracy was not significant when judgments made in assessing truthful and deceptive statements were taken together. Also, this correlation was not significant for the deceptive accounts. However, confidence and accuracy in judging truthful statements were significantly correlated. This was due to the positive relationship between confidence and the PJT predicted in Hypothesis 7: More confidence would be placed in judgments of truthfulness than in judgments of deceptiveness. This hypothesis was supported for the truthful statements. Then, since confidence in making truthfulness judgments was greater than confidence

in making deceptiveness judgments, an increased number of judgments of truthfulness did not only increase observers' accuracy, but also their mean confidence. That is why confidence and accuracy in judging truthful statements bore a significant correlation. Hypothesis 7 was not, however, supported for the deceptive statements. Across both kinds of statements the confidence–PJT correlation only reached a marginal significance ($p = .092$).

Contrary to our sixth prediction, the truth value of statements did not influence observers' confidence. Although DePaulo et al. (1997) reported a significant positive correlation, the individual studies included in their meta-analysis varied notoriously, ranging from .60 (Waxter, 1983) to $-.55$ (Allen & Atkinson, 1981), and including .00 (Köhnken, 1987). Also, recent research has failed to replicate this correlation (Masip, Garrido, & Herrero, 2003a). Future research should examine what variables account for these discrepancies.

Two possibilities were raised about confidence over time. The first one did not anticipate any change; the second one predicted a decrease in confidence as observers decided later. The results are ambiguous. Confidence across truthful and deceptive statements decreased over time, but this decrease reached only a marginal significance ($p = .066$). Probably, there were observers who waited to make their judgments until they were confident enough and reached this confidence at Moments 2 or 3, while others did not reach enough confidence and made low-confidence judgments at Moment 3. Although this explanation can account for the marginal trend towards a reduction over time of the mean confidence across truthful and deceptive statements, it cannot explain why, while the decrease was negligible when judging the truthful statements, it was significant ($p = .015$) when judging the deceptive ones.

Conclusions

In summary, most research findings reported in the US and North-European literature were replicated. However, most of the results were under the influence of the moment at which observers made their judgmental decision. Consistent with the idea that initial credibility judgments are made heuristically while later judgments are made in a systematic manner, the PJT decreased over time, particularly for the deceptive statements. This yielded an increase in accuracy in judging false accounts. The truth bias detected in deception research may be caused by researchers using behavioural samples that are too brief and uninformative. Finally, using the present design, the moment at which observers made their decision had only a marginal negative influence on confidence.

A limitation of this study is that participants were not randomly allocated to Moment 1, 2, or 3. Rather, they decided themselves when to make their judgments. As a result, individual differences may have influenced the results, since different people might have decided at different moments. Ongoing research is explicitly addressing this question.

Manuscript received December 2004
Revised manuscript accepted August 2005

REFERENCES

Allen, V. L., & Atkinson, M. L. (1981). Identification of spontaneous and deliberate behaviour. *Journal of Nonverbal Behaviour*, *5*, 224–237.

Bond, C. F., Jr, & DePaulo, B. M. (in press). Accuracy of deception judgments. *Personality and Social Psychology Review*.

Bond, C. F., Jr, Omar, A., Mahmoud, A., & Bonser, R. N. (1990). Lie detection across cultures. *Journal of Nonverbal Behaviour*, *14*, 189–204.

Buller, D. B., & Burgoon, J. K. (1996). Interpersonal deception theory. *Communication Theory*, *6*, 203–242.

Buller, D. B., & Burgoon, J. K. (1998). Emotional expression in the deception process. In P. A. Andersen & L. Guerrero (Eds.), *Handbook of communication and emotion. Research, theory, applications and contexts* (pp. 381–402). San Diego, CA: Academic Press.

Chaiken, S., Liberman, A., & Eagly, A. H. (1989). Heuristic and systematic processing within and beyond the persuasion context. In J. S. Uleman & J. A. Borgh (Eds.), *Unintended thought* (pp. 212–252). New York: Guilford Press.

Chen, S., & Chaiken, S. (1999). The heuristic-systematic model in its broader context. In S. Chaiken & Y. Trope (Eds.), *Dual-process theories in social psychology* (pp. 73–96). New York: Guilford Press.

Cody, M. J., Lee, W.-S., & Chao, E. Y. (1989). Telling lies: Correlates of deception among Chinese. In J. P. Forgas & J. M. Innes (Eds.), *Recent advances in social psychology. An international perspective* (pp. 359–368). Amsterdam: Elsevier.

DePaulo, B. M., Charlton, K., Cooper, H., Lindsay, J. J., & Muhlenbruck, L. (1997). The accuracy–confidence correlation in the detection of deception. *Personality and Social Psychology Review*, *1*, 346–357.

DePaulo, B. M., Stone, J. I., & Lassiter, G. D. (1985). Deceiving and detecting deceit. In B. R. Schlenker (Ed.), *The self and social life* (pp. 323–370). New York: McGraw-Hill.

DePaulo, B. M., Zuckerman, M., & Rosenthal, R. (1980). Humans as lie detectors. *Journal of Communication*, *30*, 129–139.

Feldman, R. S., Jenkins, L., & Popoola, O. (1979). Detection of deception in adults and children via facial expressions. *Child Development*, *50*, 350–355.

Fiske, S. T., & Neuberg, S. L. (1990). A continuum model of impression formation, from category-based to individuating processes: Influences of information and motivation on attention and interpretation. *Advances in Experimental Social Psychology*, *23*, 1–74.

Frank, M. G., & Ekman, P. (1997). The ability to detect deceit generalizes across different types of high-stake lies. *Journal of Personality and Social Psychology*, *72*, 1429–1439.

Gilbert, D. T. (1989). Thinking lightly about others: Automatic components of the social inference process. In J. S. Uleman & J. A. Bargh (Eds.), *Unintended thought* (pp. 189–211). New York: Guilford Press.

Gilbert, D. T., Krull, D. S., & Malone, P. S. (1990). Unbelieving the unbelievable: Some problems in the rejection of false information. *Journal of Personality and Social Psychology*, *59*, 601–613.

Gilbert, D. T., & Malone, P. S. (1995). The correspondence bias. *Psychological Bulletin*, *117*, 21–38.

Granhag, P. A., & Strömwall, L. A. (2000). "Let's go over this again…" Effects of repeated interrogations on deception detection performance. In A. Czerederecka, T. Jaskiewicz-Obydzinska & J. Wojcikiewicz (Eds.), *Forensic psychology and law. Traditional questions and new ideas* (pp. 191–196). Kraków: Institute of Forensic Research Publishers.

Granhag, P. A., & Strömwall, L. A. (2001). Deception detection based on repeated interrogations. *Legal and Criminological Psychology*, *6*, 85–101.

Greene, J. O., O'Hair, H. D., Cody, M. J., & Yen, C. (1985). Planning and control of behaviour during deception. *Human Communication Research*, *11*, 335–364.

Kalbfleisch, P. J. (1985). Accuracy in deception detection: A quantitative review (Doctoral dissertation, Michigan State University, 1986). *Dissertation Abstracts International*, *46*, 4453B.

Köhnken, G. (1987). Training police officers to detect deceptive eyewitness statements: Does it work? *Social Behaviour*, *2*, 1–17.

Kraut, R. (1980). Humans as lie detectors. Some second thoughts. *Journal of Communication*, *30*, 209–216.

Levine, T. R., Park, H. S., & McCornack, S. A. (1999). Accuracy in detecting truths and lies: Documenting the "veracity effect". *Communication Monographs*, *66*, 125–144.

Masip, J., Garrido, E., & Herrero, C. (2003a). Facial appearance and judgments of credibility: The effects of facial babyishness and age on statement credibility. *Genetic, Social, and General Psychology Monographs*, *129*, 269–311.

Masip, J., Garrido, E., & Herrero, C. (2003b). When did you conclude she was lying? The impact of the moment the decision about the sender's veracity is made and the sender's facial appearance on police officers' credibility judgments. *Journal of Credibility Assessment and Witness Psychology*, *4*, 1–36.

Masip, J., Garrido, E., & Herrero, C. (2004). The nonverbal approach to the detection of deception: Judgmental accuracy. *Psychology in Spain*, *8*, 48–59.

Millar, M. G., & Millar, K. (1997). The effects of cognitive capacity and suspicion on truth bias. *Communication Research, 24*, 556–570.

Miller, G. R., & Stiff, J. B. (1993). *Deceptive communication*. Newbury Park, CA: Sage.

O'Sullivan, M. (2003). The fundamental attribution error in detecting deception: The boy-who-cried-wolf effect. *Personality and Social Psychology Bulletin, 29*, 1316–1327.

Ruby, C. L., & Brigham, J. C. (1997). The usefulness of the Criteria-Based Content Analysis technique in distinguishing between truthful and fabricated allegations. A critical review. *Psychology, Public Policy, and Law, 3*, 705–737.

Stiff, J. B., Kim, H. J., & Ramesh, C. N. (1992). Truth biases and aroused suspicion in relational deception. *Communication Research, 19*, 326–345.

Trope, J. (1986). Identification and inferential processes in dispositional attribution. *Psychological Review, 93*, 239–257.

Vrij, A. (2000). *Detecting lies and deceit. The psychology of lying and the implications for professional practice.* Chichester, UK: Wiley.

Vrij, A., & Winkel, F. W. (1991). Cultural patterns in Dutch and Surinam nonverbal behaviour: An analysis of simulated police/citizen encounters. *Journal of Nonverbal Behaviour, 15*, 169–184.

Watzlawick, P., Beavin, J. H., & Jackson, D. D. (1967). *Pragmatics of human communication*. New York: Norton.

Waxter, P. H. (1983). Emotional deceit: False words versus false action. *Motivation and Emotion, 7*, 365–376.

Zuckerman, M., DeFrank, R. S., Hall, J. A., Larrace, D. T., & Rosenthal, R. (1979). Facial and vocal cues of deception and honesty. *Journal of Experimental Social Psychology, 15*, 378–396.

Zuckerman, M., DePaulo, B. M., & Rosenthal, R. (1981). Verbal and nonverbal communication of deception. *Advances in Experimental Social Psychology, 14*, 1–59.

INTERNATIONAL JOURNAL OF PSYCHOLOGY, 2006, 41 (4), 320

Psychology Press
Taylor & Francis Group

INTERNATIONAL PLATFORM FOR PSYCHOLOGISTS

Congresses and scientific meetings

August 2 - 5, 2006
11th International Society for Justice Research Conference
Berlin, GERMANY
URL: www.isjr2006.org

August 10 - 13, 2006
114th Annual Convention of the American Psychological Association (APA)
New Orleans, Louisiana, USA
URL: www.apa.org/convention

August 18 - 20, 2006
First Annual Convention, Asian Psychology Association (APsyA)
Bali, INDONESIA
URL: www.apsya.org

August 29 - September 1, 2006
XIXth Congress of the International Association of Empirical Aesthetics
Avignon, FRANCE
Contact: Daniel Jacobi, University of Avignon

August 30 - September 2, 2006
6th Francophone Conference of Social Psychology
Grenoble, FRANCE
URL: www.lps.univ-savoie.fr/CIPSLF/

September 11 - 13, 2006
37th European Mathematical Psychology Group meeting
Brest, FRANCE
URL: http://conferences.enst-bretagne.fr/empg2006

September 21 – 23 2006
First Biennial Symposium on Personality and Social Psychology
Warsaw, POLAND
URL: www.bspsp.swps.edu.pl

September 26 - 30, 2006
Joint Conference of the Australian Psychological Society and New Zealand Psychological Society
Aukland, NEW ZEALAND
URL: www.psychology.org.au

September 27 - 30, 2006
8th International Congress on the Study of Behavior
Santiago de Compostela, SPAIN
URL: http://www.ciec2006.com

October 1 - 5, 2006
Human Factors & Ergonomics Society (HFES) Annual Meeting
Baltimore, Maryland, USA
URL: www.hfes.org/web/HFESMeetings/meetings.html

October 2 - 6, 2006
Regional Congress of the Inter-American Society of Psychology, sponsored by The Cuban Society of Psychology and the Inter-American Society of Psychology (SIP)
Havana City, CUBA
Email: sip2006@infomed.sld.cu

October 4 - 7, 2006
International Family Therapy Association World Congress
Reykjavik, ICELAND
URL: www.ifta-familytherapy.org

October 11 - 13, 2006
4th World Conference on the Promotion of Mental Health and Prevention of Mental and Behavioral Disorders: "Developing Resilience and Strength Across the Life Span"
Oslo, NORWAY
URL: www.worldconference2006.no
Deadline for abstracts in March 31

October 16 - 20, 2006
Human Factors & Ergonomics Society (HFES) Annual Meeting
San Francisco, California, USA
URL: www.hfes.org/web/HFESMeetings/meetings.html

October 18 - 22, 2006
29th National Conference of the Australian Association for Cognitive and Behavioural Therapy
Sydney, AUSTRALIA
URL: www.aacbt.org.au/Conference/index.htm

October 19 - 21, 2006
14th International Conference on Eating Disorders
Alpbach, Tyrol, AUSTRIA
URL: www.netzwerk-essstoerungen.at

* Please send details of forthcoming events as far in advance as is possible to Dr Merry Bullock, Deputy Secretary-General, International Union of Psychological Science and Associate Editor of the *International Journal of Psychology*, Science Directorate, APA, 750 First Street NE, Washington DC 20002, USA; E-mail: mbullock@apa.org; URL: http://www.iupsys.org

DOI: 10.1080/00207590600775721